Reading Steinbeck:
Of Mice and Men and *The Grapes of Wrath*

READING STEINBECK

OF MICE AND MEN,
AND THE GRAPES OF WRATH

A Literature Insight

BY DAVID HALLARD

HEB ☼ **Humanities-Ebooks, LLP**

The Author has asserted his right to be identified as the author of this Work in accordance with the Copyright, Designs and Patents Act 1988.

First published by *Humanities-Ebooks, LLP,*
Tirril Hall, Tirril, Penrith CA10 2JE

Cover image © the author

The Pdf Ebook is available to private purchasers from http://www.humanities-ebooks.co.uk or from Google Play, and to libraries from Ebrary.

Other digital versions are available from Amazon and from Humanities-Ebooks.

ISBN 978-1-84760-368-5 Pdf Ebook
ISBN 978-1-84760-371-5 Paperback
ISBN 978-1-84760-370-8 Kindle Ebook

Contents

1. Introduction

Written amidst the tumult of the 1930s, *Of Mice and Men* (*Of Mice*) and *The Grapes of Wrath* (*The Grapes*) are the novels that powered John Steinbeck to international acclaim. Amongst the features that they share are the American Dream, industrialization in agriculture, the battle of the sexes, environmental concerns, and disability. Aspects of similarity include Biblical allegory (*Of Mice* is compared with the story of Cain and Abel in the book of Genesis; and *The Grapes* with the flight of the Israelites in Exodus). In *Of Mice*, eugenics is a prominent theme, whereas in *The Grapes*, the concern is evolution. Both texts discuss the Law, with *The Grapes* examining the claim that it rests on broad societal consensus; and *Of Mice* finding it to be largely absent from the lives of the agricultural labourer. The clearest difference between the two books is the respective socio-political context to which they are addressed. In *Of Mice*, set in the period preceding the Wall Street Crash, it is German militarism and the rise of fascism. In *The Grapes*, it is, of course, the Great Depression, and the consequences therein for the small farmer of the mid-West.

1.1 Of Mice and Men

Of Mice and Men is Steinbeck's hymn to a flawed humanity. His characters toil under multiple burdens, with Lennie, George, Curley's Wife, Candy and Crooks presented as the modern day *Sons of Cain*. Denied any effective personal relations, their lonely souls subsist on the meagre ration of *jam tomorrow*. The commonly held dream, their *American Dream*, is for a plot of land to farm for themselves. However, the harshest fact of ranch life is that they will never be permitted to attain it. Amidst a generalized condition of poverty, Steinbeck focuses on the particular experience of women, the African

American and people with disability. Curley's wife is defined by her marriage to the extent that she doesn't merit a signifier beyond that which connects her to her husband; and Crooks raises questions that require the unspooling of narratives that conceal America's racism for an answer. Candy, like Crooks, suffered crippling injury at the ranch and embodies, therefore, the perils that industrialism held for agricultural labourers whilst Lennie, whose life was safeguarded by the maternal love of his late guardian, is destroyed by a juggernaut of prejudice.

The American Dream is subject to considerable discussion in this book, with many characters revealing as their ideal the bindlestiff prayer for 'a little lan''. George is a source of great interest in this respect because he has yet to decide finally where his heart lies. He shares with Lennie the object of purchasing a small farm, but when the strain of caring for his friend becomes too great, he gives voice to a more selfish ambition, that of the carefree batchelor seeking sensual gratification.[1]

The strength with which he and Lennie identify with their dream marks their relationship as unique within the community of the ranch. As a form of entertainment and celebration of their endeavour, they recite an incantation which describes how they differ and what it is they wish to achieve. In its stylized execution and repetition, it resembles the refrain, a formal feature of Epic poetry.[2]

It is often observed that *Of Mice* is an allegory of the Old Testament story of Cain and Abel (Genesis: 4). Broadly speaking, there are three areas of similarity. The first is the symmetrical comparison whereby two males (in the Bible they are brothers) live together with one committing the murder of the other. The second is the extent to which siblings in general are beholden to one another. When Cain is challenged by God as to the whereabouts of his deceased brother, his answer, 'Am I my brother's keeper?', casts him as a villain; in Steinbeck's version there is ambivalence throughout as to George's

1   Joseph Fontenrose, *The Dream of Independance,* in J. Karson, ed. *Readings on 'Of Mice and Men'. The Greenhaven Press Literary Companion to American Literature.* (San Diego: The Greenhaven Press, 1998), 35–39, 37–38.
2   Leo Gurko, *The War Between Good and Evil,* in Karson, J., ed. 1998.

commitment to Lennie. The final point is the punishment meted out to Cain. Forbidden to raise a crop from the land, he is condemned to wander the earth as a fugitive. The phrase 'sons of Cain' is often applied to agricultural workers in this novel. They must also wander, leading an itinerant lifestyle according to the work that is available and like Cain, their labour is absorbed as a commodity, the profit of the harvest going into the pockets of their employer.

The prominent positioning of the reference to the Robert Burns poem announces, as an intertextual connection, clues as to Steinbeck's intentions with this novel.[1] Written in the voice of the ploughman, a patriarchal figure, the poem describes the distress caused to a mouse when her nest is upended by the plough. Through eight verses the theme is developed, from the initial recognition of fault, through the guilt of the ploughman, to an appraisal of the mouse's circumstances. The fleeting nature of the crisis, whilst a source of optimism for the mouse, is noted with regret by the ploughman, who is unable to find solace in either the past or the future.

George and Lennie's story is also one of a nest disturbed. Aunt Clara, Lennie's guardian, instigated their relationship as a shield for her vulnerable charge. As a maternal act, however, it is at odds with the exclusively male industrial ranch. As the story unfolds, it becomes clear that, like the mouse in the poem, Aunt Clara's preparations will be undone, an obstacle in the way of a masculine process seemingly blind to all but profit.

The story is set in the period before the Great Depression. Preceding the exodus from the mid-West to California, the itinerant labour force of agriculture was stable and there were few, if any, industrial disputes. It was also a time when fascism in America, through the *Ku Klux Klan*, was at its strongest. In short, this was a period when the leaders of agriculture in California, a marvel of human ingenuity and resource, could drive their project forward with scant regard for anything other than financial success. *Of Mice and Men* provides a microcosm of their world in this period. Tracing similarities between ranch life in California

---

1   Robert Burns, 'To a Mouse. On Turning Her up With the Plough', November 1785.

and the dictatorships of Hitler, Mussolini and Franco, Steinbeck offers a broad hint at the disaster invited by the cult of the father figure and the pursuit of profit at the expense of compassion.

Eugenics, the theoretical basis for the Nazi Party's *Holocaust*, was also an influence on public policy in the United States, particularly in California, from the late nineteenth century onwards. The application of scientific breeding to humanity, supposedly to remove from the gene pool the hereditary causes of disease and deformity, underpinned the Federal Immigration Act of 1882. Unlike the Nazis, however, eugenics in the USA was confined to exclusion and sterilization, with the Act barring from America any 'lunatic, idiot, or any person unable to take care of himself or herself without becoming a public charge'.[1] With regards to sterilization, more than 30 000 fell victim, over half of whom were in California. In the context of the novel, we see that Lennie, with his obvious difficulties, would not have been permitted entry to the country and Curley's wife would also have been in danger, as most of those sterilized were women whose sexual character had been challenged.

Steinbeck's publicly stated intention to produce a *Play-Novelette* was sufficiently radical as to require considerable innovation in and of itself. In traditional Realism, the all-seeing, all-knowing power of the third-person omniscient narrator affords writers a resource of some scope, but for Steinbeck, only those aspects which would transfer to the stage could be used. Dispensing with the traditional narrator, he expands the stage worthy features of the text to compensate. Of course, it is dialogue which bears the greatest burden of transmission and the result is a rich multi-voicedness. But we must also laud his use of space, the tailoring of location to enhance action, and incidental features such as the effects of light and shade and the background noise from animals and people which give emphasis to what is taking place.

1   Victoria Brignell, *When America Believed in Eugenics*. https://www.newstatesman.com/society/2010/12/disabled—america—immigration.

1.2 The Grapes of Wrath

At the time of publication, the literary merit of *The Grapes of Wrath* was, to a large extent, overlooked. Widely proscribed, it divided opinion along partisan lines, with volley fire from opposing political camps taking the place of meaningful literary discussion. Reading the novel in the twenty-first century we are, thankfully, free from such hothousing and may savour the marvels of Steinbeck's writing to the full. But it does have to be said, and I make no apology for doing so, that to have read the book as an act of solidarity, to have answered the call in the heady days of 1939 and rallied, as no other readership has, to the cause of the dispossessed, was a rare privilege and one that we look back to with envy.

Politically, *The Grapes* is not the call to arms we may have assumed, given the controversy that accompanied its publication. What we read instead is, on the one hand, an explanation of the plight of the small farmer forced into a migrant lifestyle, and on the other, a warning to the economic elite that the failure to deal with the dustbowl crisis in a humanitarian fashion would result in widespread rebellion. Steinbeck was a *New Deal* Democrat; his radicalism, such as it was, had been forced by first-hand encounters with migrant workers whose ill-treatment, he thought, to be a brazen abuse of the US Constitution.

In challenging economic times, there can be no better textual companion. The appeal for *One-Nation* government, of the duty of care for all citizens, rings clear throughout. Too often the poor find themselves as the scapegoat for economic failure. This book states in unequivocal terms that the common people are amongst a nation's most precious resources. At a time when Roosevelt's *New Deal for American People* roused the Depression-era population, Steinbeck sliced through pretence with his novel. Corrupt practices and the naked exploitation of the workforce were anathema to the government message, but Steinbeck showed just how much was yet to be done if political commitment was to be translated into social progress.

As in *Of Mice*, Steinbeck makes considerable use of Biblical reference in this book. I refer to the work done by Joseph Fontenrose, who in turn credits Peter Lisca, in tracing the numerous Biblical connections.[1] For the purpose of introduction, I include here a sketch of the principal allegory, the flight of the Israelites from Pharaoh's Egypt. The story has three distinct episodes, each of which is identifiable in Steinbeck's novel. The first, in Egypt, shows how the Israelites, persecuted by the authorities, were forced to flee. The second describes their journey to Canaan, a land promised by God. The third is the arrival in the promised land, where they must accept a new code for living and where the native population is hostile towards them.

In comparison, the small farmers of the mid-West are persecuted by the big growers and the banks, who are prepared to use martial methods against them. The plague and pestilence that God inflicts on Egypt is matched by the dust cloud, which also destroys crops and brings darkness. Likewise, the journey in *The Grapes* is fraught with hazard, but the determined Joads manage to complete it. The third part, Canaan in the Bible and California in the novel, may well be a promised land but it is also unwelcoming on account of its people. There is also the challenge of a new way of life. In the Bible, the Israelites are given the *Ten Commandments*; in *The Grapes*, hardship schools the migrants in a more socialized way of living.

Many read *The Grapes* as proof of Darwin's theory of evolution.[2] The Joad family, facing ruin, is forced to re-evaluate its outlook and practices in order to survive. The process involves conflict, and the battle of the sexes and class-struggle feature prominently in their journey. In *Of Mice* we saw the crushing of femininity, but in this novel, the tables are turned as the incomparable Ma Joad takes the helm. Allied to this is Steinbeck's defence of working-class organization and by the end of the book, we detect a collectivist, matriarchal version of the American Dream. This marks a change of some magnitude for the Joads, whose militant independence had once defined them. Steinbeck also questions the assumption that the

1 Jospeh Fontenrose, *John Steinbeck*. New York: Barnes and Noble, 1963, in B. A. Heavilin, ed., *The Critical Response to John Steinbeck's 'The Grapes of Wrath'*. (London: Greenwood Press, 2000) 67–83.).

2 Brian E. Railsback, *The Darwinian 'Grapes of Wrath'* in Heavilin, 221–231.

economic elite are a product of evolutionary development. Business is a dirty word in this book and through his account of migrant life, Steinbeck inverts the canonical narratives of economics that underpin the social order.

In terms of style, *The Grapes* is impressionistic, it is Dialogic and can even be read as a Postmodernist novel. The characters are at once memorable and convincing and in Ma and Tom Joad, protagonists who stand tall in the American popular imagination. *The Grapes* has also a distinct symbolic dimension, which plays a vital role in the transmission of meaning.

Sprinkled throughout the text, the explanatory or *intercalary* chapters house the narrative of contemporary history. As a source of fact, these chapters inform the text with the same level of authority as the narrator of traditional Realism. In his descriptions of people, it is with the dispassionate, analytical gaze of the anthropologist that Steinbeck views events; there is a sense of typicality, where the idiosyncrasies of the individual are put to one side in favour of a generalized, aggregate impression. This aspect of the intercalaries is enhanced by the use of Free Indirect Style (FIS). This technique inserts the speech of characters into the narrator's report without identifying it as such with quotation marks. When reading FIS we recognize it as speech, but because it is held within the narrator's report, it has no tie to any particular character, dispersing the comment, therefore, across the wider group.

2. Biographical and Social Context

John Steinbeck was born in Salinas, California, in 1902 and died in New York City in 1968. He was awarded the National Book Award for Fiction in 1939, the Pullitzer Prize in 1940, the Liberty Cross, by King Haakon VII of Norway in 1946 (for his contribution to the Resistance with *The Moon is Down*), the Nobel Prize for Literature in 1962 and the Presidential Medal of Freedom in 1964. He married three times and was a father to two sons.

2.1 Childhood and the Family Home

John Steinbeck had a distinctly American background which made of him, in the era that his nation found its feet as the world's leading power, truly, a man of his times. His upbringing was comfortably middle class, with a father well-respected as a manager, and a mother who combined her role as an energetic, fastidious and somewhat domineering parent with charitable efforts in town. Steinbeck was also greatly influenced by his maternal grandfather, Samuel Hamilton. A larger-than-life figure, he had migrated to America from Ireland and succeeded in farming in California where many before had failed.

Steinbeck got off to a strong start at school and came to be known as a writer and teller of stories. By all accounts, he was quite a character in his youth and this quote from Toby Street, a friend from Stanford, gives an idea of what it must have been like to encounter him at the time:

> he was like a big storm, a whirlwind. You stopped whatever you were doing and you listened to his stories. He knew how to make you listen—it was the same talent that made him a great writer.

2.2 Young Adulthood

Steinbeck's young adulthood is perhaps best thought of as a *dark night* interlude between the feminine dominions of mother and first wife. A period of self-exploration, it featured the alarmingly radical refusal to follow the official curriculum at Stanford University (he preferred instead to pursue only that knowledge which he found to be of interest) and extended periods of menial, physically demanding employment that he was obliged to undertake in order to pay his way. Still nurturing the ambition to write, he was seduced by the draw of New York City, and between spells as a maintenance man at the tourist resort of Lake Tahoe he set-sail in November 1925 to work his passage via the Panama Canal. Whilst in New York, he experienced back-breaking toil at the Madison Square Garden construction site, emotional heartbreak from romance with a Broadway showgirl, dismissal from a news reporter's job, and to cap it all, the disappointment of rejection from a publisher on the very eve of the publication of his short stories. With his resources at a low ebb, he had little choice other than to retreat and returned home to California to take stock.

He was dismissed from his position at Lake Tahoe for drunkenness, but having met his bride-to-be Carol Henning amongst the visitors that Summer, it was clear to him what his next move must be. Making his way to San Francisco, Steinbeck tracked down his girl and they compensated for the unglamorous work he was forced to take by carousing the nights away in the cheap hostelries of the Waterfront District (it was the jazz age after all). The joys of romance and a hectic social life aside, Steinbeck knew that his viability as a writer depended upon him refining his craft; buoyed by limited financial help from his father and Carol's support (she assumed many of his mother's duties during their relationship), he set to the task.

2.3 Early Struggles as a Writer

The modest success of his first novel, *Cup of Gold*, which sold its initial print-run of fifteen hundred copies, provided a timely reassurance and added to the great good fortune Steinbeck felt at having made the acquaintance of a man who was to greatly influence his outlook and writing, the scientist Ed Ricketts. Ricketts was at home amongst the culturally diverse community of the Waterfront area of Monterey and through him Steinbeck was able to add to the store of characters and tales he had already accumulated. *The Pastures of Heaven* roused neither critical interest nor significant sales, and tragically, both of Steinbeck's parents became seriously ill at this time. In 1933, the young couple moved into the family home, with the redoubtable Carol committing herself unstintingly to the cause, adding the nurse's role to her duties as housekeeper, typist and proof-reader of Steinbeck's work. *To a God Unknown* appeared in the November of this year, but again, there was little more than a lukewarm critical response. With his next effort, however, he did turn the corner, though the success of *Tortilla Flat*, which was published in 1935, was tempered by the passing of both of his parents, the source of a great and enduring sadness.

2.4 The Spur of Success

Steinbeck was by nature temperamentally inclined towards the underdog and the arrival of large numbers of displaced farmers and their families in Salinas fired both his passion and his creative energy. The 1930s had seen the growth of the *Muck-raking* novel, so-called for the narrative of exploitation authors such as Upton Sinclair and Sherwood Anderson had spun into narratives of social inequality. By the middle of the decade, however, which was indicative of the heating-up of class-relations in the USA at the time, these novels were surpassed in their radicalism by texts purporting to be the direct report of worker-activists. Magazines such as *New Masses* and *The New Republic* crackled, as it were, with the invective of the barricades. Steinbeck was enlivened in this element, pursuing stories and character profiles for his fiction amongst the displaced people of the migration. On hearing the whereabouts of two fugitive labour union activists, for instance, he arranged a meeting, making a cash offer for their story of the Bakersfield cotton strike of 1933. Their testimony gave Steinbeck an intimate understanding of the activist's role in the labour union, which he used to great effect in the novel *In Dubious Battle* (1936). With the publication of *Tortilla Flat* (*TF*), which made the bestseller list and $4 000 from the sale of film rights, Steinbeck became a hot property. For he and Carol, however, whose marriage had been a hand-to-mouth existence thus far, the royalty cheque from *TF* presented an opportunity that was not to be missed. Turning their backs on the publicity, they set off for Mexico in the Fall of 1935 for a trip which lasted until Christmas. *In Dubious Battle* was published in January of the following year and was well-received by the critics. It was now that Steinbeck turned to *Of Mice*, which appeared in February, 1937, and sold more than 117 000 copies in the first month of sale.

As far back as 1935, Steinbeck had begun to formulate his ideas for the novel which would eventually become *The Grapes*, a 'big book' which '"would be a very grave attempt to do a first-rate piece of work"'.[1] With *Of Mice* complete, this now became his focus.

2.5 Steinbeck and the Migrants

Unlike many Californians, Steinbeck had the heart to empathise with the down-on-their-luck inhabitants of *Little Oklahoma*. His hitherto working life on ranches and factories in the Salinas area, bringing him into contact with people from many different backgrounds, proved excellent preparation for the mighty task that lay ahead.

Outraged by what he saw, Steinbeck committed himself to the migrant's cause, making five separate forays into their world between 1936 and 1938. Before he had completed *Of Mice*, Steinbeck was approached by George West from the *San Francisco News* who asked if he would write a series of articles describing their experience. Steinbeck responded with the acquisition of a dilapidated commercial vehicle, the 'pie-wagon', which he fitted out for sleeping and cooking and set off for a tour of California's migrant camps. He produced

---

1 Benson, Jackson, J., *The True Adventures of John Steinbeck, Writer. A Biography* (New York: Viking Penguin, 1990 [1984]), 316.

seven articles, discussing different aspects of the situation, which were printed in the *News* during October, 1936, and which were subsequently re-published by the Simon J. Lubin society of San Francisco.[1]

Whilst on this trip, Steinbeck made the acquaintance of Tom Collins, the manager of the government camp at Weedpatch. A man of commitment and integrity, he accompanied Steinbeck for several days as he travelled, allowing him access to the many detailed reports he had compiled about the migrants. It is he whom the character of Jim Rawley in *The Grapes* is based.

When he returned home from the tour, Steinbeck was keen to start writing, but the situation surrounding the Salinas lettuce-picker strike, which had begun at the end of August, 1936, captured his attention. Little short of a localized martial law had been imposed to break the strike. Neither state nor central government were prepared to intervene effectively and an infuriated Steinbeck railed against the unfettered vigilantism that ran amok in his hometown. He fully expected an outbreak of revolutionary disorder and the anger and shame he felt took possession of his creative faculties. It is presumed that at this point he was attempting to write the 'big book' that he had first thought of in 1935, but his efforts resulted in a manuscript entitled *L'Affaire Lettuceberg*, a satire so caustic that Steinbeck burnt it, with the encouragement of his wife Carol, for lacking the literary merit his ambition for the project demanded.

2.6 The 'Big Book': *The Grapes of Wrath*

During the Summer of 1937, the situation in the San Joaquin Valley worsened and in the next few months a sequence of events unfolded which provided models for many of the more harrowing passages in *The Grapes*. 70 000 migrants had gathered in the San Joaquin Valley, most of whom were without any means of subsistence. In October, Steinbeck, accompanied by Tom Collins, set off on a month-long

---

1 These articles are listed in the Bibliography as *The Harvest Gypsies: On the Road to 'The Grapes of Wrath'*.

fact-finding tour of the camps. By Winter, it was said that there were 50 000 workers destitute and starving there.

In February 1938, there was a flood at Visalia and Steinbeck and Collins set off again. Unable to navigate the roads, the pie-wagon was abandoned to the mud and the journey completed on foot. They were met with a scene of apocalyptic magnitude, with the destitute people lying prostrate at the mercy of the elements. The two men worked continuously for forty-eight hours, fighting to save lives; Steinbeck eventually collapsing through exhaustion. They remained for over a week, giving everything they had to help the desperate and broken people. After going home for two days, Steinbeck went back for another week, this time with the intention of producing an article for *Life* magazine, who also supplied a photographer, Horace Bristol. Unfortunately, *Life* didn't publish because Steinbeck would not consent to their editing of his work, which they considered to be too broad for their readership's taste.

Undeterred, Steinbeck turned again to the 'big book' and quite miraculously, the ideas for its innovative structure, style and even controversial ending, came in a moment of inspiration.[1] It is recorded that when writing *The Grapes*, Steinbeck entered an almost trance-like state, and when it was complete, both he and Carol (who proofread the manuscript as Steinbeck wrote it) came down with heavy colds.[2] He began writing at the end of May and the first draft was completed by December. By the publication date of April, 1939, expectations for the novel were so high that the advanced order for sales topped 90 000. By the end of 1939, 430 000 copies had been sold, making it a publishing phenomenon. The film rights went for $75 000, which up to that point was one of the highest prices paid. *The Grapes* has never been out of print, nor has it sold fewer than 50,000 copies in any one year.

1   Jay Parini, *John Steinbeck: A Biography* (London: Reed Consumer Books, 1994) 248-249.
2   Parini, 252, 264.

2.7 The Great Depression

On *Black Thursday*, 24 October, 1929, the financial fortunes of the United States of America tumbled over a precipice as the optimism of the *Roaring Twenties* dissipated into the uncertainty, confusion and fear of large-scale business collapse. In 1930, 1,352 banks failed, taking $853m. in deposits with them. In 1931, 2,294 with $1.7bn.. In 1930, 26,355 businesses failed and in 1931 28,285. The total value of farm property declined from $57.7bn. in 1929 to $51.8bn. in 1931, and at the end of 1931, unemployment stood at 8m., but rose within months to 12m..[1]

The government of the day was led by Herbert Hoover, whose firm belief it was that the American people, through their hard work and resourcefulness, would reverse the crisis and set the nation once again on the path to prosperity. The national character was seen to be the country's most precious resource and needed to be shielded from the corrosive effects of state interference in the personal domain. Despite the ever-increasing number of people who found themselves in poverty, Hoover resisted calls for the state to issue relief, declaring that all such matters were to be handled locally, either by the authorities or by charities. The result was a haphazard, unregulated effort, with a diverse array of groups coming to the fore across the country. In Seattle, for instance, it was the Unemployed Citizens League who took the initiative, organizing the distribution of food and other necessities. In Philadelphia it was the wealthy whose generosity swelled the coffers of relief, following public appeals.

In the Winter of 1931, Hoover claimed that 'No one is going hungry and no one need go hungry or cold'.[2] For the many thousands destitute and starving in the *Hooverville* camps, this smacked, if not of indifference, then certainly ignorance, of their plight. The mood turned to anger. Unlike the previous decade, the 1930s was a time when radical currents could break the surface of political life, and it was

1   T. H. Watkins, *The Great Depression: America in the 1930s* (Boston: Little Brown and Company, 1993), 55.
2   Watkins, 56.

this reservoir of discontent that fuelled them. It was also a time when labour unions would lead enormous struggles, establishing themselves as legitimate organizations with whom employers were compelled to negotiate. Above all, however, it was the growth in size and influence of the Communist Party which caused the greatest concern.

2.8 The Communist Party

Between 1930 and 1933, a wave of industrial militancy broke across the USA which inspired a very real fear amongst the well-to-do. It was not yet two decades since the Bolshevik Revolution and the rapidity with which the Communist Party was attracting support suggested a similar experience was in the offing for Americans.[1]

For the Communists, the immediate objective was the domination of the labour movement. Their principal tactic was the use of the front organization, that is, organizations which functioned in the interest of the Communist Party, but were not formally acknowledged to do so. The Trades Union Unity League (TUUL) was one of the most successful and during the thirties was the means by which the Communists radicalized large swathes of the workers' movement. It had been noted that many were excluded from labour unions because they did not hold the relevant trade qualifications. By successfully campaigning for the inclusion of semi and unskilled workers, they transformed a conservative-led organization with short-term objectives into a mass force for militancy and social change. Seeing a similar opportunity with the unemployed, they combined the immediate benefits of the soup-kitchen with the promise of future prosperity through their organization, presented in the form of the Unemployed Council.[2] Among the more conspicuous of their successes was the organization of Mexican-American workers in the Imperial and San Joaquin Valleys in California. As well as low-pay and poor working conditions, these people were also subject to racial abuse, an aggravating factor that made their organization all the more impressive.[3]

---

1   Watkins, 81-2.
2   Watkins, 83.
3   Watkins, 86.

Through the efforts of individuals such as Estelle Milner in the Croppers and Farm Workers' Union and Eulah Gray in the Sharecroppers' Union (both in Tallapoosa County, Alabama), the Communist Party took the fight into the rural South, bringing behind the banner of organized labour a whole new section of the workforce.[1] A flexible approach and receptiveness to opportunity were the hallmarks of Communist activity. In the campaign to support the 'Scottsboro Boys' (a group of young African American men wrongfully convicted of rape and assault), for instance, the Communists provided legal resources through their International Labor Defence (ILD) and made use of TUUL and the League of Struggle for Negro Rights (LSNR) to publicize the cause. Over a period of six years, during which time there were many Court hearings, significant public sympathy was drummed up and numerous celebrities came forward to express their support. Finally, each of the accused were released in a landmark victory over racist oppression.[2]

Despite the tremendous efforts of rank-and-file American Communists, which flew in the face of the Communist International under Stalin, the traditional home of Labour remained the Democratic Party. Shaken by the economic crisis and the impact of the Communist Party, the Democrats were forced to reinvent themselves. The Presidential election of 1932 heralded a new period for the Democratic Party, as indeed it did for the American people as a whole.

2.9 Roosevelt and the New Deal

The failure of Herbert Hoover's administration to deal effectively with the economy, the spread of poverty and the menace of the Communist Party, brought to power the Democratic Governor of New York City, Franklin Delano Roosevelt. His *New Deal* for America was a radically different approach to the government of the United States. With a level of state intervention thus far unheard of, he sought to mobilize the

---

1   Watkins, 88.
2   Watkins, 89-91.

nation, as in times of war, to bring an end to the economic crisis. The twin aspects of the *New Deal* were the legislative initiatives aimed at making life in America a more just experience, and a programme of public works that would absorb the pool of unemployed labour for the upgrading of the country's physical infrastructure. *The National Industrial Recovery Act (Titles I and II)* laid out a social and economic plan for recovery, its Public Works Administration (PWA) financing 34, 508 projects in six years at a cost of $6 bn. The PWA modernised facilities and extended the benefits of civilization to communities hitherto bypassed.[1] Despite the ambition of the project, however, there were those amongst the workforce who would fare badly under the *New Deal* and none more so than the tenant-farmers and share-croppers of the mid-West and South.

2.10 The Dustbowl

The poor farming practices of careless ploughing and the over grazing of cattle had exhausted the topsoil of the mid-West, leaving it vulnerable to wind and water erosion. With strong winds, large quantities of dust were scooped into the air, forming clouds that blocked out the sun before descending to coat everything in sight. Steinbeck describes this process in the opening chapter of *The Grapes*. The storm that raged from 9th to 11th May, 1934, for instance, took 350m tons of soil from the West and deposited it in the East; Chicago recorded 4 lbs for each member of its population![2] This was an ecological disaster, and the cumulative effects of an extended drought, the collapse in crop prices, and the localised abuse of the *New Deal's Agricultural Adjustment Administration (AAA)*, meant that a human one was soon to follow. The mechanised technology to farm with greater efficiency was now to be had and the removal of the tenant farmer allowed for a more profitable enterprise for landlords.

The *AAA* operated a scarcity programme which Steinbeck discusses to great effect in Chapter Twenty-Five of *The Grapes*. In order to

---

1   Watkins, 142–144.
2   Watkins, 192.

maintain the price of goods in the shops, farmers were encouraged to destroy any crop which would create a surplus. Locally, however, under the administration of the landlords, the tenants and croppers were swindled out of both the compensation provided by the scheme and their shares. A national policy which was dedicated to their assistance resulted in many of them being forced from the land. Between 1930 and 1935, 20% of farms in the mid-West, Central South and the Plains were foreclosed. In 1933, unemployment in Arkansas stood at 39% and in Missouri, Oklahoma and Texas, between 29 and 32%; Oklahoma lost 440 000 people during the 1930s.[1]

Since the Goldrush, California had been a magnet for migrant workers. Between 1910 and 1930, approximately 300,000 from the South West had made their way there and for those now finding themselves displaced it was an obvious destination. Many went to the urban centres of Los Angeles, San Francisco and San Diego, but there was resistance to them from the authorities, particularly in Los Angeles, where the repatriation policy against Mexican-Americans could just as well have been applied to the migrants. Those who did not wish to live in the cities were absorbed by the itinerant labour pool of agriculture, which swelled in size to 300,000, over 20% of whom were located in the San Joaquin Valley.[2]

2.11 Struggle in California

Agriculture had achieved many great things in California, but as an ongoing concern, its dependance upon low wages made for a fraught regime. The great fear of the growers was Communism, but in the attempt to insulate themselves, they gave opportunity to those who would cynically exploit the *red scare* for their own ends. Squeezing Constitutional rights, taking unfair advantage in commerce and the use of excessive violence in industrial disputes became acceptable in the face of the perceived threat from the left.

Following the victorious strike of 15 000 cotton-pickers in 1933,

---

1   Watkins, 193-194.
2   Watkins, 195-198.

the big growers resolved to organize their response to future militancy. The Associated Farmers (A.F.) was the result and through its activities, came to be synonymous with intimidation. Amid a flux of union agitation and the radicalization of the Democratic Party, Steinbeck's book provided a textual focus, a talisman for the opposition to the big growers. With its hackles raised, the A.F. swung into action, determined to neutralize the influence of *The Grapes of Wrath*.

2.12 The Struggle for *The Grapes of Wrath*

The A.F. Campaign brought pressure to bear in two ways. First was a challenge to the factual accuracy of the book. This took the form of a publicly conducted line-by-line audit of the text to the accompaniment of books and films dedicated to a contradictory version of events. Secondly, and more controversially, there was the use of prohibition, which saw the removal of the book from circulation.

To give a flavour of the times, I include here a brief account of events in the California town of Bakersfield, a place known well to Steinbeck, which stood at the centre of the storm gathering around his book. On Monday, 21 August, 1939, at a meeting of the local authority, the Kern County Board of Supervisors, it was successfully moved by Stanley Abel that *The Grapes of Wrath*, in both the book and cinematic form (the film was still at the production stage at this time), be banned for its profanity, lewdness and 'foul and obscene language'.[1] Having read the book, we know this claim to be false; however, the full weight of official authority was brought to bear in support of the ban. How could this be so? For a more satisfactory explanation, we must place the decision in the context of a nationwide trend for the banning of the book. Public libraries in Kansas City, Trenton NJ, Buffalo NY, San Francisco and Detroit all took action. In East St Louis, all copies of *The Grapes* belonging to the library were burnt and on board the USS *Tennessee*, the chaplain removed it from the shelves of the ship's library despite there being a list of fifty

---

1   R. Wartzman, *Obscene in the Extreme: the Burning and Banning of John Steinbeck's 'The Grapes of Wrath'* (New York: Public Affairs (Perseus), 2008) ,8.

people waiting to read it.[1] In the climate of censorship, *The Grapes* had become a political weapon. To read it was to participate in the struggle, to strike a blow for the poor against wealth.

The prevalence of such a censorious attitude invited comparison with Nazi Germany and in the week leading up to the next meeting of the Supervisors, public opinion caught fire. On Monday, 28 August, the Board re-convened, though in very different circumstances. The public gallery was crammed full and the atmosphere, ratcheted-up by left-wing activists coming into Bakersfield to propagandize, was charged. A sense of history-in-the-making permeated this traditionally conservative place, but the succession of speakers protesting against political censorship could not sway the reactionary Stanley Abel, whose insistence that the ban was for obscenity won the day. Following the Board's decision to ratify the ban on *The Grapes* in the teeth of a genuinely mass opposition, it became incumbent on the government to act against the A.F.[2] The Senate investigation of late 1939 provides at least some consolation for those who challenged the Supervisors' decision. Led by the reformist Republican Robert M. LaFollette, the investigation concluded that where the A.F. was able to exercise its will, a 'local fascism' was the result.[3]

The controversy surrounding *The Grapes*, and the decision to enforce localised censorship around the country, shows the extent to which Steinbeck's novel was a lightning-rod for the forces acting on the migrant issue. In spite of the specifics of its setting, it raised questions of society's structure that were universally applicable. The Kern County Supervisors' bullish refusal to rescind their decision, despite the weight of evidence to the contrary, indicates that the big growers had drawn a line in the sand on this issue. For Steinbeck, caught on the wrong side of this *line of scrimmage*, there was an enduring rancour. For the migrants, the yearned-for integration did occur, but only with the outbreak of war, when their labour power was absorbed by munitions production in the factories and shipyards of the *Golden State*.

---

1   Wartzman, 10.
2   Wartzman, 211–220.
3   Wartzman, 222.

3. Steinbeck's Literary Strategy

> A writer out of loneliness is trying to communicate like a distant star sending signals. He isn't telling or teaching or ordering. Rather he seeks to establish a relationship of meaning, of feeling, of observing. We are lonesome animals. We spend all life trying to be less lonesome. One of our ancient methods is to tell a story begging the listener to say—and to feel—"Yes, that's the way it is, or at least that's the way I feel it. You're not as alone as you thought".[1]

For Steinbeck, who was identified with storytelling from an early age, writing was an occupation that offered considerable reward in and of itself. In a letter to a friend, he describes a sense of exhilaration: 'What an extension of self is this pen. Once it is in my hand—like a wand—I stop being the confused, turgid, ugly and gross person. I am no longer the me I know'.[2] He was clearly transformed by writing and sought to preserve it as a source of empowerment. Foremost amongst hazards, as he saw it, was the commercialization of his work. In a letter to his literary agent, he stated: 'The idea of a salary doesn't appeal to me at all. I intend to write what I want to'. And: 'we've gone through too damned much trying to keep the work honest and in a state of improvement to let it slip now in consideration of a little miserable popularity'.[3] Clearly, fame came at a price that Steinbeck would not pay and the annoyance he felt with those who did is plain from another letter in which he refers to a writers' party he attended: 'They don't even pretend that there is any dignity in craftsmanship. A conversation

---

1 E Steinbeck R Wallsten, *Steinbeck: a Life in Letters* (New York: Viking, 1975), 523.
2 Parini, 89.
3 Steinbeck and Wallsten, 111.

with them sounds like an afternoon spent with a pawnbroker'.[1]

An important part of Steinbeck's philosophy was the belief that writers work in the service of civilization. In a letter from 1954, he discusses the obligation to bear witness, to inscribe in literary form the salient aspects of our day-to-day experience.

> The responses to this spectacle, whatever they are, are going to be one of the keys to our future attitudes toward everything. If such things are not written as fiction, a whole pattern of present-day thinking and feeling will be lost. We will have the records but not what people felt about them.[2]

Steinbeck's engaged writing and meticulous research certainly do justice to these sentiments, but his fastidious and single-minded approach was not universally well-received in an environment dedicated to money.

Given his determination to write exclusively from conviction, he was guilty, on occasion, of showing too little regard for publishing etiquette. This characteristic, effectively a badge of honour, also placed him at the mercy of the more cynical elements within the profession. During the rewriting of *Of Mice* for the stage, for instance, Steinbeck was suspected of a slight against George S. Kaufman, the director and producer brought in to assist with the process. Desperate to return to California to begin work on *The Grapes*, Steinbeck paid too little attention to his eminent associate, and rumours flew of a falling out. Previously, Steinbeck had caused alarm during the final preparations for *In Dubious Battle*. His publisher made the customary request for publicity material for the launch; Steinbeck claimed that 'any procedure which is designed to make a writer ego-conscious is definitely detrimental to any future work', and refused.[3] Clearly, Steinbeck's sensibility would brook no compromise, particularly with what he saw as peripheral concerns.

Steinbeck's sensitivity to publishing extended to the way in which writers are encouraged to work. In a letter to his agent in 1954, he

---

1   Steinbeck and Wallsten, 30.
2   Steinbeck and Wallsten, 485–486.
3   Parini, 193.

made the surprising admission that the lifelong attempt to shape his methods into an acknowledged signature style had been a fool's errand. What he had realized, and presumably what other writers concealed, was that such a refinement brought with it a distancing from one's subject. Rather than the careful application of technique to the specifics of circumstance, there was the abuse of a writer's privilege. Here is some of what he had to say.

> Having a technique, is it not possible that the technique not only dictates how a story is to be written but also what story is to be written? In other words, style or technique may be a straitjacket which is the destroyer of a writer. It does seem to be true that when it becomes easy to write the writing is not likely to be any good. Facility can be the greatest danger in the world.

He concludes the letter with the following sentiment, 'I want to dump my technique, to tear it right down to the ground and to start all over'.[1] This selfless and noble intention, whilst enhancing Steinbeck's standing as a committed writer, did little to endear him to his peers.

The clarity of Steinbeck's writing and the extent to which it resonates with historical circumstance, is due in no small part to the time he spent out in the field conducting research. To faithfully bear witness one must engage and from very early in his career, Steinbeck had been mindful of the value of other people's experience and anecdotes to his writing. The proximity of events that shaped the nation in the 1930s was, therefore, something of a gift to him. He lived like a news reporter, trekking the country to piece together narratives from those caught in the action. From Tom Collins (the manager of the migrant camp at Weedpatch), to Cicil McKiddie (a fugitive labour leader who was later to die in the Spanish Civil War), from the radicals discussing socialism at the John Reed Club, to the Monterey biologist Ed Ricketts, Steinbeck the distiller tapped them all.

---

1   Steinbeck and Wallsten, 497.

3.1 Steinbeck and Politics

Steinbeck's response to fascism was at once instinctual and energetic, as was his reaction to Soviet Russia. He exhibited his general dislike for 'communists' on visits to the Soviet Union and in episodes such as his disagreement with an editor, Harry Black, a Communist Party sympathiser who rejected his manuscript for *In Dubious Battle*. For the discussion of *Of Mice* and *The Grapes*, however, it is the immediate danger from fascism that provides his focus.

Whilst not an activist in the party-political sense of the term, Steinbeck was always prepared to make a personal intervention. His views were heartfelt and inspired action, not mere phrasemongering. During a scriptwriting mission for Herbert Kline in Mexico, for instance, he saw that the Nazis had established a considerable propaganda network south of the border. Wishing to relay his findings to the American authorities, he made the surprising move of writing to the President himself.[1] Despite the apparent naivety of the gesture (the CIA may not have come into existence until 1947, but American Intelligence would most certainly have been aware of the situation in Mexico), Steinbeck was granted an audience with Roosevelt in June 1940. That his proposal, for the stepping up of America's propaganda effort against Nazism seemingly fell on deaf ears, is of little surprise, but that a subsequent request to see the President in August was also granted, most certainly is. Once again, Steinbeck presented a proposal (this time for the destabilization of the German economy with vast amounts of counterfeit currency). The President listened politely, but the idea went no further. Regardless of the outcome of the discussions, one thing is certain: Steinbeck, as a committed and eloquent anti-fascist, was a world apart from the sombre-suited bureaucrats who surrounded the President. His willingness to extend, to engage with political reality, distinguished him as a writer and at a time when America's conscience was being pricked to join the war against Nazism, explains, perhaps, why he was received with such good grace at the White House.

---

1   Steinbeck and Wallsten, 206.

3.2 Writing the War

The Second World War saw Steinbeck showcasing the full repertoire of personal and technical attributes that distinguish him as a writer. With the publication of *The Moon is Down* (*The Moon*) and *Bombs Away: The Story of a Bomber Team* (*Bombs Away*) Steinbeck showed that his ability to produce texts that resonated with contemporary circumstance had not dulled. With *The Moon*, which sold more copies than *The Grapes* and saw Steinbeck decorated with state honours from the King of Norway, he produced a text which was taken to heart by those fighting in the Resistance. In a comment regarding the book (which came in for severe criticism from some in the literary world for a perceived lack of artistry), Steinbeck suggests that his tenacity as a researcher was once again instrumental in his success, 'Gradually I got to know a great deal about these secret armies and I devoted most of my energies in their direction'.[1]

Bombs Away was a commission from the US Airforce and involved Steinbeck spending a month with the new recruits to its Bomber Command, seeing first-hand the selection and training process. Once again sales were encouraging and Hollywood eagerly snapped up the film rights.

As a response to the threat that he might, despite his age, be drafted into the army, Steinbeck had sought to prove his worth to the country as a writer. His attempt to become a war correspondent, however, was almost scuppered by lobbying from the reactionary *American Legion Radical Research Bureau*. Though he overcame the obstacle, his experience showed that the need for a struggle against the far right was not confined to Europe.

As a war correspondent, Steinbeck's inventiveness inspired a brand of writing that came to be known as the *New Journalism*. Steering clear of the customary reliance on official statistics and the like, Steinbeck focused on the experience of the thing, bringing home to the reader, through his impressionistic response, how it felt to be involved. He lived with the soldiers and short of carrying a gun saw the same action as they did, even landing on shore as part of the D-Day invasion of Italy. Steinbeck's articles were printed throughout the US and Britain and in several countries of Latin America in translation. When Twentieth Century-Fox released Alfred Hitchcock's *Lifeboat* in 1944, they received a letter of complaint from Steinbeck, who had written the original script. In it he referred to alterations which had introduced elements of class and racial prejudice.[1] This was of course anathema to Steinbeck, a lifelong friend of the working-man and ally in their struggle. So strongly did he feel about the betrayal, that a month later he requested his name be removed form the film credits. In referring to Hitchcock as 'one of those incredible English middle-class snobs who really and truly despise working people', Steinbeck demonstrated that as a writer of conviction, his work and principles were as one.[2]

3.3 Steinbeck and Modernism

As the most conspicuous cultural movement of the early twentieth-century, Modernism had a profound effect on publishing. In establishing a context for Steinbeck's writing, therefore, we must be aware of Modernism both as a textual practice and as an idea of what it means to be a writer.

As the instinctual reflex of cultural production to the shock of modernity, Modernism was a decisive commitment to the values of civilization. However, the refusal of Modernists to engage in public life, particularly in politics, exposed them to the charge of elitism. Steinbeck's flair would have been fed by the creative energy and textual innovation of the Modernist project, but his profile as an engaged writer precluded any withdrawal from the everyday. This troubled relationship was not exclusive to Steinbeck, and George Orwell, who along with Christopher Isherwood had retraced a path to the traditional Realist format with a textually transparent, politically aware fiction,

---

1   Steinbeck and Wallsten, 266.
2   Steinbeck and Wallsten, 267.

observed in *Inside the Whale* (1940), that the denial of politics placed a considerable burden on the integrity of the Modernists.

I include here mention of Steinbeck's experience on the writers' committee of *People to People*, the government sponsored anti-Soviet propaganda body of the 1950s. Chaired by William Faulkner, the committee had a decidedly Modernist slant and as such, provided opportunity for comparison with Steinbeck at close-quarters. Following the unsuccessful uprising in Hungary in 1956, many of its citizens were in danger from state reprisals. Steinbeck saw an opportunity to help and urged the committee to petition the US government to organize an airlift of refugees. Though his suggestions were accepted, the other members, unaccustomed as they were to political activity, were not prepared to carry the matter to a meaningful conclusion. Steinbeck's shoulder-to-shoulder approach provided a stark contrast to his counterparts who would not extend beyond the sphere of cultural production, even when a grand humanitarian gesture was theirs for the taking. In the colloquial setting of a personal letter, Steinbeck gives a sense of the disquiet the Modernists created with their generalized policy of withdrawal.

> When these old writing boys get to talking about The Artist, meaning themselves, I want to leave the profession....They really get to living up to themselves, wrapped and shellacked. Apparently they can't have any human intercourse again.[1]

With the advance of fascism and the entrenchment of totalitarianism in the Soviet Union, the increasing likelihood of world war compelled writers of conscience to orient towards political matters. For Steinbeck, any retreat from the issues of the day was a betrayal of his craft.

3.4 The Context of Modernism

Afraid that civilized value would be lost in industrial modernity, the Modernists sought to preserve a space where subjectivity could flourish. The term Modernism relates to the commitment these artists

---

1   Steinbeck and Wallsten, 529.

had to *make new* the subjective values at the heart of Culture. Their quest to reconnect with the natural condition of human life, as the basis of the artist's subjective response, saw them reject the external, physical world and turn instead to the inner world of the emotions. They found in art what Kant had described as 'purposiveness without purpose', a sphere into which their efforts could be poured but which would not be of benefit to the despised industrial system. Art became a world in itself, featuring as a prominent theme in their work as well as a means of expression.

3.5 Features of Modernism

In its vanguard, writing in the period immediately preceding the First World War, were the *Impressionists*, Henry James, Joseph Conrad and Ford Madox Ford. In prefaces to his novels, James sketched out a manifesto which addressed what he saw as its shortcomings as an artistic form. Thematically, it was a case of highlighting the *significance* of experience, not the simulation of *slices of life*. Restricting life in the novel to the responses given by one central character, the *Impressionists* made the initial forays into a literature committed to subjectivity. As well as removing the chronologically sequential development of plot, they also dispensed with the third person omniscient narrator of traditional Realism, a development with particular interest to students of *Of Mice* and *The Grapes*.

The shift in emphasis from the external world to inner subjectivity gave memory a higher profile in the narrative scheme. Detailed recollection of past events is given greater priority, particularly when the character's attention is transported involuntarily. This feature is familiar to readers of *The Grapes*, in which the character Muley Graves is greatly affected when recollecting his past life.

Moving onto later Modernist writing, an aspect with special relevance to Steinbeck is the use of allegory. Using ancient mythology as a mine of transcendent value, they created a juxtaposition with the prevailing norms of the day. In *Of Mice* and *The Grapes*, it is the Bible to which Steinbeck turns as his prominent frame of reference.

3.6 Active Reading Technique

Another feature of Modernist writing with specific interest is the demand for an active reading technique. Traditionally, the burden of comprehension was shouldered by the writer. In Realist writing, the reader understands that the meaning inscribed by the author is fixed and will be accessible through the transparent presentation of character and event. For the Modernists, this encouraged a passive, unreflective way of reading which they sought to discourage. Their readers were to interrogate the text with rigour, seeking out meaning from an increasingly ingenious textual practice.

Like the Modernists, Steinbeck placed the onus for meaning creation with the reader who must make sense of the surface detail he provides of behaviour and circumstance. He had this to say, for instance, of *The Grapes*, 'There are five layers in this book, a reader will find as many as he can and he won't find more than he has in himself'.[1]

3.7 Steinbeck the Impressionist

In the manner of the *Impressionists*, Steinbeck exercised his subjective response without recourse to the obvious structures of authorial omniscience. As Ford Madox Ford had pointed out, 'the Impressionist author is sedulous to avoid letting his personality appear in the course of his book. On the other hand, his whole book, his whole poem is merely an expression of his personality'.[2]

In the following examples from *Of Mice*, we sense the challenge that Steinbeck presents to his reader, probing their worldly knowledge with the sparseness of his 'expression'. As Lennie and George come into view for the first time, we are informed that they 'wore black shapeless hats';[3] in the river, 'reeds jerked slightly in the current';[4]

1 Steinbeck, E. and Wallsten, R., 1975. P178—9.
2 Ford, F.M.. On Impressionism (1914). In Baker, W. and Womack, K. eds.The Good Soldier: a Tale of Passion. Ontario: Broadview, 2003 (1915). P260—280. P269.
3 Steinbeck, J., Of Mice and Men. London: Penguin Pocket Classic, 2006. P2.
4 Steinbeck, J., 2006. P8.

when Lennie fights with Curley, 'Curley was flopping like a fish on a line';[1] and similarly, when Lennie kills Curley's wife, 'her body flopped like a fish'.[2] The 'shapeless hats' reference is particularly audacious, but in the description of the reeds, the phrasing is such that we wonder that anyone who has not observed this phenomenon first-hand will appreciate its accuracy. Of the similes connected with angling, again, there is no embellishment of the sensory impression recorded. For a country boy like Steinbeck the sight of a 'fish on a line' would have been a common enough occurrence, but it would not have been for someone who had spent their entire life in an industrial town in Pennsylvania, for instance. The demystifying propensity of television was a prospect for the future and the amount of experience covered by Hollywood at this point would not have sustained any substantive transcultural comparison. We should be mindful of the advantage afforded by the proliferation of information in our age and understand that for the contemporary reader, Steinbeck was as stern a taskmaster as his Modernist counterparts.

3.8 Breaking New Ground

In a letter from 1937, Steinbeck admitted that, 'I've broken every literary rule when I wanted to'.[3] It was very much in this spirit that *Of Mice* was written, a novel that could double as a stage play 'as it is'.[4] In 1933, Steinbeck had this to say of his novella *The Red Pony*, 'The whole thing is as simply told as though it came out of the boy's mind although there is no going into the boy's mind. It is an attempt to make the reader create the boy's mind for himself'.[5] Here we see Steinbeck use his impressionistic style to expand his reader's understanding, giving the text a consciousness-raising quality. What is true for *The Red Pony* is also true for *Of Mice* in this instance, which was also written without an omniscient narrator. During the

---

1   Steinbeck, J., 2006, 71.
2   Steinbeck, 2006. 103.
3   Steinbeck and Wallsten, 137.
4   Benson, 325–326.
5   Steinbeck and Wallsten, 71.

early stages of writing *Of Mice*, Steinbeck expressed the intention, 'to create a child's world, not of fairies and giants but of colours more clear than they are to adults, of tastes more sharp and of the queer heart-breaking feelings that overwhelm children in a moment'.[1] We know, of course, that it is not a novel for children, but the attempt to stimulate the receptiveness of childhood in the reader shows a clear commitment to both impressionism and the expansion of his reader's understanding.

Of course, a text can be consciousness-raising only if it is read by those whom it is meant to benefit. It was widely understood that working men did not read novels, but if Steinbeck were to succeed with his *Play-Novelette*, he would not merely have created a new format, he would also have brought into the community of readers an important group thus far excluded. The *Aztec Circus* had staged daily theatrical shows for striking cotton workers in California, but success for Steinbeck would have been of a different order. In May, 1937, the *Theatre Union* performed *Of Mice* for sixteen nights at the Green Street Theatre, North Beach. Unfortunately, Steinbeck was persuaded that as a play, his book fell short of the standard set by professional playwrights. The dedicated stage version certainly did satisfy criteria, however, and Steinbeck's message was heard by packed houses across the nation.

It was with the 'symphonic technique' he employs in *The Grapes* that Steinbeck makes his boldest statement as an impressionist. In a letter of February, 1939, he had this to say, 'I have worked in a musical technique … and have tried to use the forms and the mathematics of music rather than those of prose…. In composition, in movement, in tone and in scope it is symphonic'.[2] In *Working Days*, there are two entries which flesh out our understanding of what he meant. On 4th June, 1938, he wrote, 'the next chapter tells of the coming of the tractors and must have a symphonic overtone'.[3] Then on 7th June:

---

1   Benson, 325–326.
2   Steinbeck, Letter to Merle Armitage, 17 February 1939, in R. DeMott, ed. *Working Days: the Journals of 'The Grapes of Wrath' 1938–1941* (New York: Penguin, 1990 [1989]).13.
3   DeMott, 22.

> Today's work is the overtone of the tractors, the men who run
> them, the men they displace, the sound of them, the smell of
> them. I've got to get this over. Got to because this one's tone is
> very important—this is the eviction sound and the tonal reason
> for the movement.[1]

The idea that a text may be onomatopoeic, that each individual
chapter will possess a distinct tone which corresponds to the message
imparted, is a development of some significance and shows once
again Steinbeck's propensity for innovation.

3.9 Steinbeck's Dialogism

A favourite of Steinbeck was Fyodor Dostoevsky, a pioneer of the
polyphonic or Dialogic novel. Seeking a representation of character
which was free from the taint of authorial point-of-view, Dostoevsky
dispensed with many of the props of traditional Realism. Giving their
word the same weight as that of the author/narrator, his characters
are played, one against another, in highly-charged set-piece episodes,
in which the key issues of the text are resolved in an atmosphere of
excited multi-voicedness. Steinbeck's task with the *Play-Novelette*
was to find new ways of communicating meaning, in his Dialogic
novels, Dostoevsky had pointed the way.

3.10 The Idea

The currency of Dialogism is the idea. Characters are drawn to ideas
which give definition and expression to their innermost selves and
with which they become synonymous. They are not, however, merely
the embodiment of an idea and for much of the time this cherished
inner-belief remains concealed. The signature idea exerts profound
influence and compels the host to represent it with the fullest of force
in the dialogic exchange between characters. What we witness in
these seemingly uncharacteristic outbursts is the overwhelming of the
character's socially-constructed persona (the psychological vehicle

---

1   DeMott, 23.

by which they navigate society) by their inner, emotional core.

Following these episodes, we are able to attribute a human identity, a face, to a particular idea. This is a very important aspect of Dialogism, the means by which the writer flags key issues: only ideas with sufficient potency to take possession of a character and propel them beyond the routine of their normal lives have this standing. At the roadside, in Chapter Sixteen of *The Grapes*, for instance, the idea of family unity takes the paradoxical form of Ma Joad threatening her husband with an iron bar.

A reading of *Of Mice* highlights, above all, the consequences for George and those near to him, of his not having committed to a signature idea. In a situation where he is pitched together with characters who positively burst with belief and commitment, it is a shortcoming of the utmost seriousness. The two dreams he has inscribed in poetic refrains, the farm dream he shares with Lennie and the bachelor's ideal of the carefree pursuit of pleasure, pull George from different directions; the action of the story providing the experience that forces his hand.

4. Sequential Development and Analysis

4.1 Of Mice and Men

Chapter 1

The reader may find a little fanciful the dedication of the opening passage to natural history, given the themes Steinbeck develops in this book. However, on closer investigation we see that the description of the riverine environment is used to introduce one of the big drivers of the narrative.

It is likely that the details selected for comment have arisen from Steinbeck's first-hand observation. For instance, would someone who had not spent time at the riverside mention the temperature of the water and debris fouling the branches of trees? We also note that he sought an explanation for what he sees. If the river runs deeply and is shaded from the sun, what is the explanation for the high temperature of the water? And how did flotsam become entangled in the branches? The term consciousness-raising is often applied to this work, and from the very first page we see that finding answers to questions, the ladder of the process, is a habit the author encourages us to develop.

One of the more impressive structural features of the book is the amount of information Steinbeck imparts through dialogue. Whilst appearing to be the natural conversation of working-men, it is in fact a finely crafted matrix of references, tying the story to the prominent social, cultural and political narratives of the day. In this chapter, the emphasis is on introduction.

We learn very quickly that Lennie has some sort of learning disability and that he is dependent upon George. The obsession with a dead mouse, and George's insistence that he remain silent when they reach their destination, confirms the problem to be of some magnitude. We are also told that Aunt Clara, of whom George is mindful in his care of Lennie, indulged his passion for mice; that Lennie was prone to killing these poor creatures portends much of the gruesome incident that is to follow. We should also note that the discussion concerning their previous job foretells the outcome of the plot: Lennie, unable to control his urges, roughly manhandles a young woman, albeit unintentionally and they are forced to flee.

Chapter 2

The conversation between George, Lennie and Candy provides an insight into life on the ranch. Candy performs the essential diplomatic task; attending to newcomers, he calms their suspicions and reduces the likelihood of their taking fright and leaving.

By the end of the chapter we have encountered all of the characters (excepting Crooks and Whit) with the Boss making his sole appearance. We learn more about Lennie and George and find that two men travelling together, with one acting as spokesman for the other, is controversial and rouses suspicion. We see that the Boss's son, who is not, as one would expect, his right-hand man, is recently married to a young woman whose sexual morality has been called into question. This worsens the anger he habitually displays and adds to his menace as a bully, making of his marriage both a public exhibition and a comedy.

Steinbeck's Unreliable Narrator

The discrepancy between objective situation and narrator's report, which occurs throughout, indicates to the reader that in this book, the narrator is what is termed *unreliable*. A rhetorical tool used to generate irony, here, the narrator's expression of sympathy to the Boss, though understated, is at odds with Steinbeck's theme and must, therefore, be treated with suspicion.

In keeping with the ethos of *agribusiness*, the plot develops rapidly and the narration, restricted to the seemingly dispassionate sketching of surface detail, threatens to carry our attention past information crucial to a firm grasp of the text. The report of the interior of the bunkhouse, for instance, though detailed, fails to shepherd the reader to the obvious conclusion: that it is a rudimentary, meanly equipped shelter that offers little by way of comfort and even less of privacy. Instead, we are distracted by the misleading use of wholesome sounding adjectives such as 'long', 'whitewashed' and 'solid', and the suggestion, with the inventory of personal effects crammed into the apple-box shelving, that the men enjoy the privilege of accumulating possessions.

Accepting that Steinbeck's narrator is not the fount of meaning, we must be alert to the techniques used to compensate. Dialogue is the foremost vehicle, but in this chapter we also get a sense of how space is used to provide a meaningful ambience to the action.

The Boss

It is entirely in keeping with his rarefied position that the Boss should make just one brief appearance in the book, a tantalizing glimpse of an individual whose power and influence are absolute. From the details of his attire and physique we learn that he is 'not a labouring man'. We also see that he is possessed of a sensibility that is offended by what he learns in the interview with Lennie and George. In the first instance, we note that the marks of his position are slight in comparison with the ostentatious displays of wealth evident in the television dramas of today's American West. A high heel and a spur on a boot are not much by way of acknowledgment of authority and indicate the level at which his operation runs. If the Boss turns out in such workaday fashion, is it likely that his business will sustain the cushion of a corporate management culture or charter for workers' rights?

The set-up is patriarchy in its barest form. Headed by the Boss, the workforce is a pecking order which must follow his lead. With regard to his sensibility, we find it surprising that, given the anonymity one would anticipate in a workplace reliant on casual and itinerant labour, the Boss should take such a keen interest in Lennie and George. For whatever reason, his suspicions are roused by the simple fact that there are two men on his ranch who are bonded in a relationship based on care.

George

We learn in this chapter something of George's fallibility, particularly his limitation as a carer for Lennie. His fatal error is to believe that he can pursue his own agenda whilst at the ranch. Considering our observations of the Boss and the obedience he demands, we cannot help but think that George is heading for trouble.

One of the more obvious of George's characteristics is that he is readily aggressive. Rounding on Lennie for having spoken in front of the Boss, he gives the impression of being overly harsh. The use of the adjective 'viciously' in the narrator's report confirms the fault. He also turns on Candy, whom he has caught eavesdropping. The speed with which he asserts himself indicates more than a short temper, however, and is an early indication of George's refusal to accept the discipline of the workplace hierarchy. On the ranch, the regular workforce, those who are not likely to transfer their services elsewhere, are the Boss's people, and any challenge to them is a challenge to his authority.

Whilst running little risk with the diplomatic Candy, the same could not be said of Curley. As the Boss's son he enjoys privilege, and for George to speak to him 'coldly' in their first meeting, and on his return, 'coldly' again, and worse still, 'insultingly', shows a cavalier disregard for etiquette. Gut instinct or not, it is confirmation that George is susceptible to egotism.

George gives further cause for concern when he is told by Candy of Curley's reputation as a boxer and bully, particularly of taller men with whom he frequently picks fights. Surprisingly, given his instruction to Lennie to maintain a low profile, and the narrow escape at their previous employment, George's suggestion that Curley will come off worst if he tackles Lennie indicates a mind-set insufficiently attuned to circumstance. Despite Candy's further efforts to placate George, making it plain that as the Boss's son, Curley cannot lose when he picks a fight, George's reiteration of the boast confirms his misreading of the situation. On the riverbank he had sufficient awareness to drill Lennie on the basic rules by which they were to survive, but here, he fails to apprehend the very great danger they face.

When Candy departs and George and Lennie are alone together, George again displays weakness in his reasoning. He acknowledges that if there is a fight between Curley and Lennie, they will be dismissed, but rather than leave and find somewhere else to work, he tells Lennie to keep away from Curley. Having set his sights on earning $100 from the job, he is either unwilling or unable to reconsider. Given their experience at Weed, George should have made discretion the better part of valour. He runs through the escape routine with Lennie, but should he really have faith in his companion's ability to follow it in the event of an emergency? We see that George is capable of reasoned thinking and that he possesses worldly knowledge, but he is far too sensitive to perceived slights to his self-esteem to take proper care of his friend.

Curley's Wife

It is perhaps with regard to Curley's wife that the unreliability of the narrator is most apparent. The transmission of plain fact without embellishment gives a suspiciously restrained impression of this provocative young woman. When she first appears, for instance, there is a sense that she has stage-managed the episode. Immediately preceding her entrance a wagon pulls up at the bunkhouse; George and Lennie would have understood this to mean the arrival of workmen, not the young wife of the Boss's son. Their surprise at seeing her is excited by the dynamism of her presence. Standing on the threshold, her appearance is overtly seductive. Whilst it is not remarked upon by the narrator, her actions describe a feminine invasion of masculine space and an incident of some magnitude. As the conversation develops, it is left to the reader to apprehend the sexual charge of the episode for themselves. The narrator's comments, 'said playfully' and 'smiled archly and twitched her body' describe acts of flirtation, but are not noted as such.[1]

George and Curley's Wife

Curley's wife gifts George the opportunity to exhibit a worldly-wise character. The swiftness with which he confirms the consensus that she is a 'tramp', and his comments about Curley's vaseline treatment and impotence regime, raise his profile in the bunkhouse. However, he also shows his fallibility, and his handling of Lennie's very obvious attraction to the young woman falls well short of what the situation demands.

For a man who leads a hand-to-mouth existence, George seems very inflexible at times. The interest shown by Lennie in Curley's wife, in light of their experience at Weed, should have alerted him to the hopelessness of their position and prompted an immediate departure. His failure to do so indicates a serious fault. It should also be noted that Lennie pleads with George to leave but is told that they must stay.

Slim

A worker-aristocrat and right-hand man to the Boss, Slim is the embodiment of masculine hegemony in the bunkhouse. Abandoning reticence, the narrator swoons over the 'prince of the ranch', acknowledging his dexterity, gravitas, wisdom, and a burgeoning authority that radiates beyond the confines of his work.[2] Like Curley, Slim echoes the Boss's suspicions, but unlike him, he conducts himself with a quiet dignity, displaying the perspicacity and assuredness of the professional master of men. Drawing George in with friendliness, he gently but persistently presses for the information sought. His is the competent interrogation, the engagement with George that will furnish the Boss with the knowledge he needs to satisfy his curiosity.

---

1   Steinbeck, 2006, 35.
2   Steinbeck, 2006, 37.

Chapter 3

This chapter is the first in which the dark undercurrents of this pressurised environment break surface in violent incident. Following a hard day in the field, the lowering light in the bunkhouse indicates rest for the weary men. However, when Slim switches on the lamp it is apparent that for him at least, the working day is not yet complete. For George, this chapter makes increasingly clear his shortcomings both as a man and as a carer for Lennie. Beginning with his emasculation before Slim's 'Godlike eyes' and embarrassed fumbling on being found out by Candy, his mood swings to elation as it emerges that they have the money to buy a farm. His joy is, of course, short-lived, and the fight between Curley and Lennie plunges him back into turmoil.

Slim

That there is more to Slim's occupation than 'buckin' barley' is made abundantly clear in this chapter. Predicting the Hollywood staple of the interrogation scene, the beam of the lamp excludes all but he and George as the task of obtaining answers to questions first raised by the Boss begins in earnest. Taking care not to trigger George's defences, he gives him every encouragement to confess. In repeatedly referring to Lennie in complementary terms, he assuages George's concerns, but with a comment about guys who become so disaffected that they shun conversation, he inserts a moral barrier which prevents George from curtailing his outpouring. Slim presses home his advantage with consummate articulation. His lofty position at the ranch is confirmed by the clamour to back him as he remonstrates with Curley; Carlson is surprisingly aggressive and even the lowly Candy weighs in with a disparaging remark about the Boss's son.

George

Having asserted himself with Candy and Curley, George finds Slim an altogether different proposition. Irresistibly, the leading hand brings pressure to bear and George unburdens himself of his backstory. His indiscretion is not confined to the conversation with Slim; his embarrassed response on finding Curley eavesdropping also adds to our disappointment.

George's response, on hearing that Lennie is interfering with the puppies, signals another capitulation. Having sought to establish exclusive rights of communication with Lennie thus far, he now surrenders them, inviting Slim to deal with the problem rather than go to the stables himself. We also note that the language he uses when referring to Lennie is not appropriate, given his professed commitment to care for his friend.

When talking to Whit, George is invited to accompany the other hands when they visit a *cathouse* in town. Given the circumstances, he should decline the offer; he is, after all, saving money and should not leave the vulnerable Lennie to his own devices. In not doing so, George gives further cause for concern, which he then aggravates with contradictory instructions for his friend. Whilst on the one hand he drums into Lennie the need for him to stay out of trouble (to the extent of not speaking to anyone), he also forbids him from taking a beating from Curley. For a man of Lennie's limitations this poses a cognitive problem of some magnitude.

Carlson

Briefly introduced in the preceding chapter, Carlson is revealed to be a callous and manipulative presence. Like Slim in the conversation with George, his comments about Candy's dog were not off-the-cuff but the opening gambit in a psychological ploy. We see him roll out his initiative to destroy the ailing canine with the careful preparation and timing of his argument, the calling forth of supporting testimony, and the physical means by which the deed is to be carried out. A key moment, in which the suspicions we have of this sinister character crystallize, is the announcement that he has 'Got a Luger'. Reverberating through the text, this news connects Carlson with

German militarism and the Nazi Party.[1] The Luger automatic pistol had been a staple of the German military since the Great War and offers, therefore, a metonym of some strength here. As the men await the gunshot, the silence and tension in the bunkhouse indicate an event of great seriousness. Whilst Candy's feelings would have been respected by his fellows, there is the suspicion that an issue of greater importance than the euthanizing of an aged canine is at play. The connection with Nazism made by Carlson and his Luger pistol has charged the occasion, the generalized anxiety of a world on the brink of war channelled through an incident on a ranch in California.

Metonymy

With metonymy, Steinbeck conjures a tangible sense of foreboding that bewitches his characters and compels his reader to acknowledge an emerging threat. Metonymy is defined as 'a figure of speech that replaces the name of one thing with the name of something else closely associated with it'.[2] Where metaphor functions on similarity, metonymy stipulates connectedness. Metaphor gives space for comparison, for interpretation, metonymy does not. It describes a closed circuit of motive and purpose, the *on* phase of a binary with no intermediate or *maybe* position. On the ranch, where a lack of choice is the defining feature of life, the symbolic value of the Luger designates it, like the hangman's noose or the guillotine, as the recognized implement of execution.

Curley

Curley's marriage, like the *Keystone Kops*, consists of a seemingly endless chase sequence and earns him, quite naturally, the ridicule of his fellow workers. His aggression is well known and, combined with the hypersensitivity he exhibits about his wife, indicates the

---

1   L. Owens, 'Deadly Kids, Stinking Dogs, and Heroes: the Best Laid Plans in Steinbeck's 'Of Mice and Men'' in *Steinbeck Studies*, Fall, 2002.

2   C. Baldick, *The Concise Oxford Dictionary of Literary Terms* (Oxford: Oxford University Press, 1991) P135.

likelihood of violence at some point. However, Curley is not immune to hierarchical law and comes unstuck when he challenges Slim. Taking on senior figures is a risky business and even more so in this case, where Slim occupies a position that should have been his. In an extraordinary scene, where he finds himself facing the entire bunkhouse, Curley desperately attempts to save face with an assault on Lennie, a man who, despite being much larger than he, was not expected to fight back. The smaller man's much-heralded pugilistic skills are in evidence as he pummels the hapless Lennie, but the fight ends abruptly when his victim defends himself. The injury sustained by Curley, whilst grotesque and life-changing in its severity, is not shocking in the sense that it is unexpected. There is a palpable sense of danger at the ranch and the loss of a limb is very much an occupational hazard.

Chapter 4

This chapter stages a concert of voices that would, as a matter of course, be suppressed by the regime of the ranch. Whilst Crooks's room is actually a part of the stables, the fact that it is known to be his gives it a certain autonomy. This distancing, whilst provoking the envy of the ranch-hands, also supports a freedom, a confidence to express, that is not possible elsewhere. It is understandable from the Boss's point of view that the other hands are prohibited entry. Crooks's room appears to be the one place on the ranch where a sincere personal discussion may be held, making it the ideal setting for the multi-voiced exchange we see here. Crooks, Lennie, Candy and Curley's wife engage in a discussion remarkable for the intensity of feeling it conveys. Peeling back the layers of cynicism, Steinbeck negotiates the many inconsistencies in his characters' beliefs and actions to reveal a hope that is common to them all: the bindlestiff yearning for a plot of land and escape from the curse of Cain.

We know that the unreliable narrator is a source of irony which equates, in this book, with sympathy for the Boss. As we enter Crooks's domain, therefore, a space charged with political significance as the special accommodation of the African American, our suspicions keen at the narrator's comment. As we read the description of Crooks's room and possessions, a disparity is again evident between what is reported and the objective situation. If Crooks is so fortunate, why is his personal space taken up with equipment for the livestock? And is it not ironic, when we read the list of his belongings, that a man who is forced to live with beasts may own so many accessories to civilized living? What is the narrator concealing? The reference to Crooks as a 'proud, aloof man' suggests haughtiness, but we know that he has suffered violent assault whilst at the ranch. Could it be that the narrator's report creates an impression of Crooks that eases the idea of segregation on racial grounds? If Crooks dislikes the company of others, the Boss has done him a favour by accommodating him separately. Steinbeck shows here how racial segregation may be explained away as a matter of everyday expediency, of good housekeeping. The skills and knowledge that Crooks possesses make him a valuable resource, but as an African American he cannot be seen to be treated as an equal to the other hands. In this pared down model of the social order, it is entirely predictable that the solitary African American will be subject to violent abuse and estrangement, the hallmarks of a segregated society.

It is of little wonder, given the violent subjugation of the African American, that Crooks's comments, when taken as a whole, do not form a coherent *voice*. His remarks are disjointed and produce a fragmented, idiosyncratic discourse which, confusingly, keys into seemingly random aspects of the African American experience. Given the collective history of persecution and exploitation, of extermination and the destruction of origins, we must understand that Crooks, as the embodiment of black experience, could sound in no other way and still remain convincing.

On inviting Lennie into his room, he commences a sadistic game. Assuming a proprietorial air, which is accentuated by the spectacles he wears for the occasion, he quite mercilessly attempts to unsettle his guest, combining barely decipherable statements about loneliness and the value of human company with the prospect of George abandoning him. Crooks stops only when Lennie presents himself as a physical threat, the end of the game signalled by the removal of the spectacles.

Steinbeck makes clear that Crooks has a middle-class, Californian identity. Unlike the African Americans who fled the South in the Great Migration, the farm where he was born was owned by his father. However, from his comments, it is not at all clear how he has arrived at his present predicament. When he was a boy, his father disapproved of him playing with white children. Crooks did not understand why at the time, but intimates that he has since learnt. We know that the *Ku Klux Klan*, the principal focus of white racism in America in this period, attained a membership of some nine millions by 1924. We also know that California was one of its strongholds, its members rampant in their persecution of any who opposed, or did not conform, to their ideals. Perhaps in mentioning this, Crooks is admitting that the segregation he is subjected to on the ranch is not the first time that white racist bigots have compromised his life.

Though he lives separately, Crooks is still a member of the ranch community. As widespread as the dream of land for oneself is the refusal to believe that it may ever be attained. Crooks shows his connection to the ranch with both his cynicism about the chances of the others, and enthusiasm when convinced of the possibility of success. His offer to work without pay has historical connotations for the African American and proves that the dream must burn at least as brightly for him as it does for the others.

Having gathered momentum, the mood of optimism is shattered by the intervention of the white female. Steinbeck's account of the felling of Crooks's nascent aspirations, at the very instant at which they appear, provides a salutary reminder of the hostility faced by the African American at this time. Teased out of his shell by the unthreatening Lennie, and further encouraged by the old man Candy, he is at his most vulnerable. On the entrance of Curley's wife, Crooks sees danger and attempts evasion in a 'terrible protective dignity'.[1] He is, however, unable to weather the storm, and in rising to his feet to expel the invasive presence, is poleaxed with a tirade

---

1   Steinbeck, 2006, 89.

of abuse. Curley's wife's attack resonates with the racial violence that historically underpinned the American social order. As a white woman, her power over the African American is absolute, her word sufficient for the taking of his life. In a stronghold of the *Klan*, her threat to have Crooks lynched could not be taken lightly and signals the end of his involvement in the purchase of the farm.

In a text noted for its shocking content, this episode has grown in potency as time has elapsed. The advances made by the African American community, along with the entrenchment of multiculturalist values in public life, has blurred the memory of the not-so-distant past. The readiness with which Curley's wife launches her attack, however, confirms that nakedly racist behaviour such as this was once considered the norm. With so few options in life, the poor white woman clings to the oppression of the African American, an affirmation of racial identity which gives at least some sense of personal worth. Curley's wife's humanity, the paradox of a living person that can inspire, on the one hand, a wholeheartedly feminist sympathy, has, by the end of the chapter, caused revulsion.

The Curse of Cain and Steinbeck's Dialogism

With his meticulously staged polyphony, Steinbeck speculates on the curse of Cain as a generalized condition amongst the poor of North America. Crooks, Candy and Curley's wife give voice to their experience of the enforced solitude and impoverishment that the curse entails. By careful presentation, each of the voices is heard as a distinct force, there is no conflation into group consciousness, nor privileging of social position, which gives the impression, in the flow of the reading experience, of equality in suffering.

For Crooks, loneliness has been a blight. Excluded from the society of the ranch, his experience of solitude has been one of disorientation. When talking to Lennie, he describes unease at not having anyone to hand who could confirm his experience. He recalls his youth, a time when he was surrounded by family and never wanted for a living soul to agree or disagree with, to confirm or deny, something he may have seen or thought. His contemptuous dismissal of the farm idea provokes an impassioned and resolute response from Candy, who describes his own burden under the curse as a ceaseless toiling for a harvest that can never be his. Crooks is taken aback somewhat by Candy's response. The elderly man's heartfelt insistence strikes a chord with the African American, who admits that he had never yet seen the dream come to fruition. Candy repeats this display of bravado when Curley's wife sneeringly dismisses the plan; a splendidly Dialogic example of the transformative power of ideas, even in lives as humble as these. This is the moment where the optimism inspired by George and Lennie's plan reaches a peak, the possibility of escape reversing all of the negativity thus far expressed.

The arrival of Curley's wife shatters the fellowship of the men. Exuding sexual appeal she voices her displeasure at being confined to the company of males not sufficiently sprightly for a jaunt in town. Opening her heart on the poor white woman's take on the curse, we see that her experience is in some ways worse even than that of the African American male; at least Crooks has something in his own right. For Curley's wife, life holds nothing outside of her marriage.

Chapter 5

The industrial character of the setting in its wider sense is hammered home in this chapter. All aspects of life on the ranch are dedicated to the Boss's economic purpose; like a machine, each must integrate or be dispensed with. This is the law and there can be no exceptions. Incidentally imparted detail contributes greatly to the generation of atmosphere, with the shapes made by light, the noise from the horses' halters, the buzzing of flies and the sounds from the horseshoe game acting as a coded orchestration.

The first human death in the story is predicted with the killing of the puppy by Lennie. Unable to comprehend death, Lennie talks to the creature as though it were still alive. His concern is soon overtaken, however, by the realization that he will not now be trusted with the rabbits they had planned for the farm. Comprehending this fact is a bitter blow for Lennie, who contrives to deceive George into thinking that the puppy had died naturally.

The thought of Curley's seductively dressed wife sidling up to Lennie rouses conflicting emotions. We feel for Lennie, whose experience of women up to this point has yet to extend to romance. We see that in all likelihood he is being played for selfish reasons. She would not normally see him as a match, as a young woman with allure why would she? We know that he has been chased out of town following an incident with a woman so we fear the worst. The suspicions roused by Curley's wife are, however, tempered by the knowledge that she is also one of the victims of the ranch; embittered by the hand life has dealt her, she lives as a prisoner.

Unlike Crooks's room, the barn is not a place where dissent can be expressed. Curley's wife's confession about her marriage is a transgression which carries a high level of risk. Irritated by the restrictions that George has imposed on Lennie, she blurts out her story of missed opportunity in show business. She genuinely believes that she has the potential to be an actress. She talks of the men who sowed the seeds of illusion in her mind, unscrupulous men who sensed her susceptibility to flattery of this kind. In confessing that she married Curley to get away from her mother, however, she oversteps the mark and we sense that she must now face some form of retributive discipline. Despite coming to the conclusion that Lennie is 'nuts', she does not leave him; her loneliness and craving for attention overwhelm her good sense, forcing the fatal error of inviting Lennie to caress her hair.

Lennie answers the question as to why he is 'so nuts about rabbits' in a passage of dialogue which, unlike his customary gibberish, shows him to possess discernment and a sense of proportion; he is not completely taken with imbecility, yet when he talks of his Aunt Clara and the piece of velvet, it is plain just how terrible a burden his learning difficulty is. The struggle with the woman is typical of Lennie. His impulse is to stifle, and like her husband, the woman is compared to a 'fish on a line' as she fights for her life.

Though we may have been appalled with her in Crooks's room, the image drawn of Curley's wife in death leaves us in little doubt as to her standing as a figure of sympathy. There is a sense of exaltation as silence descends. Her face, framed by the halo of her golden hair, begs comparison with a Renaissance Madonna. In keeping with the tradition of Tragedy, time stands still to mark her passing.

Cinematic

By the mid-thirties, the production of movies with soundtracks was in full swing. We know that Steinbeck was well thought of by filmmakers as his career progressed, but at this stage, as he stood on the cusp of greatness, there is another point to be made in regard to the movie industry. The passage which follows Lennie's exit is loaded with references to ambient sound. We observe that a hush falls on proceedings as the young woman's body lies undiscovered, but as we near the moment of her discovery, there is a steady increase in the volume of background noise. As in the cinema, where moments of emotional intensity are prepared by a suitable accompaniment from the soundtrack, the discovery of Curley's wife's body is heralded by noise from the horses' hooves and halter chains and the raised voices of men playing horseshoes. Ever alert to the spirit of his times, Steinbeck incorporates aspects of cinematography, keying into a new cultural development to expand the graphic aspects of his writing.

The Dream is Lost

George and Candy's discussion over the body marks the end of their dream. In answer to Candy's forlorn pleading, George recites details of the life he will lead without Lennie. He trades a dream of mutual support and cooperation for one of individualism and sensual gratification.

The remainder of the scene, in describing the response of the ranch hands to the girl's death, provides an insight into a lynch-mob culture that had been widespread in the US. With industrial efficiency, retribution is planned and a posse formed to hunt down the fugitive. We note that Slim is the first to approach the body, but Curley, the woman's husband, does not. His concern is for revenge against Lennie and the decision to shoot him is assumed rather than discussed. A fair trial in a court of law is not a consideration.

Dialogism

In a chapter in which Dialogic pressure results in murder, George's hand is finally forced and Curley's wife, at the mercy of her yearnings, loses her life. For all her brash talk and crude racism, it was not the dream of celebrity but an escape from loneliness that Curley's wife desired most. Starved of affection by her husband, and by her mother before, her craving for company forces a fatal error of judgment. The idea of stardom, a lifestyle of adoration and the attention of others is a young woman's fancy, a veil behind which the pleading for relief from the biting harshness of the curse of Cain lies concealed.

For George, whose altruism is in tatters following his interrogation by Slim, the death of Curley's wife finally ended the mutual dream of the farm. Whilst this may, superficially, have resolved his dilemma, the loss of his role with Lennie has consequences that he has not bargained for. Already in this chapter, the dream of pleasure seeking sounds hollow compared to the allure he gave it when talking to Lennie. George's tragedy is that he did not realize how much his relationship with Lennie, and the dream they shared, gave to him. The transgression elevated George, a man with contempt for authority, above the other workers. As a single man he must conform, and no amount of 'pleasure' will compensate for what he has lost.

Chapter 6

For the final chapter, we return once again to the Salinas river. Steinbeck achieves structural symmetry with the bookending of an industrial narrative by passages of natural history writing. The sense that the story is an interlude from the norm was suggested in the working title of the book, *Something that Happened.*[1]

The narrator's report of the riverbank emphasizes a change that has come about since the opening chapter. The snake, which had slipped

---

1   Parini, J., 1994. P229.

into the river as dusk approached in the earlier visit, is now devoured by the heron, a mortal peril which had initially been put to flight by the arrival of George and Lennie. Lennie himself is again compared with a bear, but on this occasion it is as a creature hounded and in fear for its life. He drinks from the river, but without the greedy abandon of the opening.

The account of Lennie's torment provides a vignette of his life following the passing of his Aunt Clara. Unable to control his impulsiveness and immense physical strength, he waits on tenterhooks for a reprieve. When George arrives it is with a sense of resignation that he addresses his friend. As the posse draws nearer, he shows no inclination to escape. Instead, he calms his friend's fears, giving no hint as to his deadly intent. Lennie's joy is a moment of pathos showing Steinbeck's flair for the macabre, a twist of the knife in the insides of a reader primed for the worst.

George goes through with the murder with only a shaking of the hand to give away the enormous emotional charge of the episode. Steinbeck stated that George is a hero, who, in taking the life of his friend, shoulders the full burden of responsibility for him.[1] This has ameliorated for some the shocking violence of the episode. However, there are others for whom the denouement suggests a symbolic event with much more sinister implications. When George walks away with Slim, his friend blown to pieces on the river bank behind him, we see capitulation and a leap along a path which led eventually to the *Holocaust*.

4.2 The Grapes of Wrath

Chapter 1

Steinbeck evokes a delicious, unearthly sense of apocalypse in this chapter, an intercalary describing the disastrous effects of the dust cloud in America's mid-West. The catastrophe is discussed as it relates to patriarchy, with the women expressing the concern that

---

1   Steinbeck, E. and Wallsten, R eds., New York, 1975. P563.

their way of life may come to an end if the menfolk are broken by their experience. The subsequent narrative may be read, therefore, as Steinbeck's attempt to give them hope, particularly through his heroine, Ma Joad.

Chapter 2

The image of the gleaming new truck, in the opening sentence, is one that haunts the narrative as the impoverished farmers inch their way Westwards in broken down jalopies. Of the three characters featured, Tom Joad is quite clearly the outsider, a feral presence tentatively feeling his way back into life as a free man. The conversation between truck skinner and waitress, whilst unexceptional and quotidian for them, is an aspect of life denied those in prison; for Tom, a casual flirtation is an event of some significance. Tom is unaware of the catastrophe that finance houses and land owning companies have inflicted on his people; in making certain that he understands the term 'tractored-out', the truck skinner prepares him for the shock that awaits.

Working-Class Life

A distinctive feature of the book that has become apparent at this point is Steinbeck's representation of the working class. Informed by first-hand experience, the warmth and sensitivity of his writing ensures a nuanced representation of this complex and diverse social group.

Steinbeck uses the conversation between the two men to make a general comment about the working class. Though he leads a relatively privileged existence compared to that of his passenger, the truck skinner, isolated from human contact in his occupation, and insulated from the hunger and poverty which defined life for many at the time, appears flabby in a psychological as well as a physical sense. Has his financial security been purchased at the expense of his mental well-being? Tom is razor-sharp; his time in gaol was spent on his wits and, despite being deprived of his liberty, seems to be the healthier of the two. In comparing the men, we see that neither is a clear winner in life; what they have been given with one hand has been taken back with the other.

Symbolism

Though a very minor player, the truck skinner contributes not only to our understanding of context, but also to the symbolic life of the book. When the bee enters the cab he is careful to steer it, unharmed, out of the window. The bee is the symbol not only of industry, fidelity and virtue, but of capital accumulation. The truck skinner prospers because he is careful with things that help him. Tom, on the other hand, instantly kills the grasshopper before ejecting its remains. The grasshopper is a symbol of good luck which gives the power to leap into ventures without preparation. Tom has inadvertently killed a friend and we may consider it a bad omen for him and his family on the road.

Chapter 3

An intercalary which discusses a law of nature that equips things which cannot move with the wherewithal to be transported from one place to another; and the land turtle, the symbol of the migration. We sense Steinbeck's great enthusiasm for natural history in the descriptive passages of this chapter. In examples such as the 'oat beards to catch on a dog's coat' and 'sow bugs like little armadillos, plodding restlessly on many tender feet', there is little trace of the biology textbook.[1] Indeed, in the *pre-information* age of black and white movies, we suspect that it was again first-hand experience that enabled Steinbeck to produce such finely drawn observations.

In a paradoxical expression of the 'anlage of movement', the land turtle inadvertently makes use of the kinetic resource of automobile traffic to cross the road. As a symbol for the migrants it has ponderous strength and an indomitable resolve to overcome disadvantage. We may also note that its journey provides a vignette of the Joad narrative.

1   J. Steinbeck, *The Grapes of Wrath* (London: Penguin Classics, 2000) 16.

Chapter 4

A narrative chapter in which Tom meets Jim Casy. The land turtle of the previous chapter seems to have transported itself between two ontologically distinct realms. From the contemporary-historical mode of the intercalary chapter, it finds itself in the fiction of the Joad narrative. It is a very obvious example of Framebreaking, a distinguishing feature of the Postmodern novel that is discussed in the chapter dedicated to Critical Reception.[1]

When Tom meets Casy and it becomes apparent that they are known to one another and will travel together, we understand that a journey of some importance has begun. Steinbeck's description of the 'anlage of movement' in the previous chapter now assumes symbolic importance: the small farmers are played out, and must move on.

Casy and Religion

Our initial impression of Jim Casy is somewhat contradictory. He has been a religious preacher and Tom recalls his innovative approach, but by his own admission he was far from the virtuous soul one associates with the calling. Indeed, the sexual misdemeanours he refers to, whilst not unknown to the established Church, are an abuse of privilege and suggest unsuitability. From the details revealed, it is plain that the religion described is unofficial and has a folk-cultural basis. The 'sperit', a psychological influence on the gatherings which prompted all manner of outlandish behaviour, so enlivened the people that one cannot help feeling that Casy is being overly harsh on himself. He points out the paradox of a force that was assumed to be Holy but which also roused wanton carnal desire in women. He admits that he now has difficulty in accepting religious scriptures as the truth. For Casy, the 'sperit' was not a holy thing but an expression of the love inherent in human communion; he knows Jesus only as a subject of stories, but the 'sperit' he has seen and felt.

---

1   B. McHale, *Postmodernist Fiction* (New York: Methuen, 1987), 197–198

Tom Joad and Prison

Tom was gaoled for killing a man in a fight. He is unrepentant and would do the same again if need be. One of the ironies of the book is that, in material terms at least, Tom would have been better off if he had remained in prison; whilst there, he had eaten well and earned the respect of his peers, even performing for them in a string band. As they walk along, Tom discusses his father and Uncle John, giving the impression that both men are prone to eccentricity and selfishness, though not with any great malevolence. As we observe in *Of Mice*, the migrants seem oblivious to the environmental harm caused by litter. The offence committed by Tom when he tosses aside an empty whisky bottle is made all the more ironic by his walking barefoot.

Chapter 5

An intercalary which describes the eviction process of the tenant farmer. The landowners in their cars and the tenants squatting to draw shapes in the soil, are again observed with the dispassionate eye of the anthropologist.

The contrast between the tenant farmer system and industrial agriculture is presented as a struggle between the human and the inhuman. The small farmer personalizes his method, imprinting a mental and physical struggle onto production. Industrial agriculture is the erasure of the personal. The use of machines obliterates the record of the human effort spent in a tradition; an algorithm with no signature, it leaves only product and waste. To emphasize the point, the comparison is made between the mechanized planting process and rape.

Anonymity is the defining feature of the corporate structure; from the top of the enterprise downwards, noone is accountable. Agency is denied by the 'owner men' who refer to their seniors as monsters. The landlords blame the banks, whom they say have forced mechanization to guarantee profit. Without names or faces to connect with decisions, the sense is of a wholly unjust disenfranchisement. The small farmers would fight if they could identify their enemy. Furthermore, they are criminalized if they resist the order to leave. The threat to use police (and even troops) against them is real and provides a wretched footnote to their way of life.

The tractor driver is offered as the human replacement for the tenant farmer. In a cyborg relationship, however, his humanity is obscured by the needs of the machine. He drives the tractor but cannot smell the ploughed earth. Ensconced in protective apparel, his skin is sealed from the environment; sitting upon an iron seat, he transmits control through unfeeling iron levers.

Symbolism

This is the first time that Steinbeck mentions iron, an element with some significance in his play of symbols. In superstition, it is used to ward away witches, but as the element of industrial modernity it is a resource of infinite malleability which gives structure and shape to civilization. In short, iron empowers the conquest of nature and we should pay close attention to the circumstances in which Steinbeck mentions it. The emphasis here is on the dispassionate application of technology for commercial gain.

There is a short passage of dialogue in this chapter which interrupts the narrator's contemporary historical report. In a snippet of first-hand reportage, the tractor driver is given the opportunity to speak. Facing the tenant farmer as he takes a break from ploughing, the driver explains how a man who hails from that community may take work which will place up to a hundred of his people in destitution.

Chapter 6

A narrative chapter which returns Tom Joad to his family's deserted home. He meets the ghost-like character of Muley Graves, a man who is unable to join the migration because he cannot face the prospect of leaving his lifelong home. Muley is a warning to Tom: to remain on the land is to exclude oneself from the ongoing story of humanity.

Casy

With the remark, 'We got to get thinkin' about doin' stuff that means somepin',[1] Casy initiates a strategy discussion on the issue of state aggression and of how the migrants may resist. He dismisses Muley's offer to disable the headlamps of the Deputy's vehicle, making clear that individual acts of vandalism are counter-productive. From his remarks, we see that Casy no longer thinks like a religious minister, though he has yet to define his new identity. All that is clear at this stage is that he feels the need to be with the people as they migrate.

Muley Graves

Muley describes a type of mental breakdown that he has suffered. Anxious about leaving, his mind has been paralysed in episodes of involuntary recollection. His awareness of the present was blocked out as he relived, in his imagination, experiences that shaped his life. Muley's conundrum is that all of these incidents took place on land that he was required to vacate. To leave would be an abandonment of a significant proportion of what he amounted to as a person. His home is, in effect, the externalisation of his inner dimension. Whilst Tom revels in the anecdotes he can relate, it is clear that he will still function when he leaves (he already has whilst in gaol).

In the previous intercalary. The tractor driver makes the point that his duty is to his immediate family, not the wider community. Muley recalls a similar conversation with his friend, Willy Feeley, who reacted angrily when asked how he could do so much harm to his own people. Again, the man driving the tractor acknowledges a duty to his family alone. This is another point we will bear in mind as the story progresses. The evolutionary advance plotted by the Joad narrative is empowered by the commitment to a more socialized way of living. The confinement of one's concerns to the nuclear family belongs to the life they leave behind.

---

1   Steinbeck, 2000, 61.

Chapter 7

An intercalary describing the painful process by which the migrants acquired the 'anlage of movement'. As if the wrench from their homeland were not enough, they now become prey to unscrupulous merchants. Steinbeck makes use of Free Indirect Style (FIS) to give a flavour of the experience.

We saw in the second chapter, with its shiny new truck, that there were vehicles in commission that would have made short work of the journey to California. However, it would appear that instead, the migration became a disposal facility for the country's stock of broken-down automobiles. As the nation mobilized for Roosevelt's *New Deal*, the migrants were trapped in the preceding regime of Herbert Hoover, with its staunch belief in the ability of the resourceful American to overcome adversity without assistance.

There are two voices in the narrator's report: the manager, or proprietor of the showroom, who addresses his salesman; and the salesman, who addresses the farmers. There is no report of the farmer's speech, which is relayed instead through the salesman's remarks. When not on their own land the tenant farmers are prey to sharp practice; they have no voice and to all intents and purposes have been criminalized. Calamity for them, however, spells bonanza for the used-car salesman. Having to raise money at short notice, the farmers are forced to sell their belongings for whatever the buyer is prepared to pay. It is an acutely unfair market: what they buy is worth less than they pay: what they sell is worth more. The farmers are trapped and they have no other option.

Chapter 8

The emotional warmth of the Joad family enters the text along with the rising sun. Tom returns to the fold as they make preparation for the journey and we encounter for the first time the force that is Ma Joad, 'the citadel of the family, the strong place that could not be taken'.[1]

---

1   Steinbeck, J., 2000. P77.

In the story of Uncle John, as told by Tom to Casy, and the description of Tom Senior, we get a sense of the harshness of the tenant farmer's life. They are men physically toughened by work but with limited perceptions. They also display symptoms of eccentricity, a fault which becomes increasingly apparent and costly as their fortunes decline. At times of great adversity, it is to the senior menfolk that the family look for guidance. However, from the earliest reports, we suspect that Tom Snr. and John will disappoint. Each carries a burden of guilt (John blames himself for his wife's premature death and Tom Snr. for his son Noah's cognitive limitations) and the suspicion is that it will prove to be too great.

Tom Joad

From the very first, Steinbeck takes care to present Tom as an example of uncompromised manhood. Thought and action flow from his personality without the complications we see in his father and Uncle John. He is a man of peasant stock whose mind has been shaped by the struggle against the elements and those who would take what is his. He does not intellectualize and he is not affected by dogmatism. His body, likewise, is ready for physical effort. When he returns to the family home, his father seeks amusement from his reintroduction, but Tom has to caution him against creating an unnecessary trauma for his mother. It is Tom who gives the mature male response in an early indication of what is to follow.

Casy

Having rejected the Gospel, Casy finds that he still has a ministry. His ideas about the totality of the human soul, and refusal to feel guilt for behaviour that is both typical and widespread, are taking him into philosophical territory that he will not discuss. When he is invited into the Joad household, for instance, the Grace he gives is unusual and certainly not of a conventional Christian type. He makes the point that holiness is not one man working for another, but of all men working for each other. He is moving toward what we would call socialism, but Steinbeck does not present him with the prepackaged option of political programme and propaganda. Instead, he is shown to go through a learning process, an organic development prompted by experience.

Grampa and Granma

The grandparents are people of the frontier. Shorn of affection, they expect to fight for what they need. Their love for family is fierce and is matched by their resolve against enemies.

Ma Joad

Like her son Tom, Ma Joad is described as having grace and poise despite a physique that bears the mark of hard, physical work. It is made plain that she is not the housewife of bourgeois respectability, but the source of strength, the bedrock upon which her family stands. Her immediate concern for Tom is that he has not been compromised by his experience in gaol. She fears for his character, that he may have become tainted with bitterness. She knows her son, she knows his qualities and the intensity with which she questions him shows her great belief in him. Casy is not alone in moving toward a collectivist point of view. Whilst talking with Tom, Ma makes the point that there are one hundred thousand people who share their predicament, and if they were to stand together, the authorities would be powerless against them.

Chapter 9

An intercalary that relays the sense of injustice felt by small farmers who were forced to sell their possessions before taking to the road. Free Indirect Speech is used extensively, but on this occasion, it is the farmer for whom the narrator speaks.

With heart-rending poignancy, Steinbeck expands the theme introduced with Muley Graves. We hear of the intensely personal experiences associated with material possession, and the loss of identity the farmers feared when either selling or burning what they were unable to carry. The pain they felt, however, was short-lived. Their fears were the fears of settlers; once on the road they were quickly forgotten as the struggle to survive absorbed all of their energies.

Chapter 10

The moment when the Joads cease to be people of the land and join the ranks of America's itinerant labour force. One by one the family find their way to Ma Joad. We begin with Tom, who shows how different he is to Muley Graves. His tour of the farm is a pilgrimage, but when completed, he is ready for the move.

Tom and his Mother Have a Special Relationship

In this early encounter between mother and son, we see that they are bonded by mutual respect and trust. As they talk, they calm each other's misgivings about the move to California. She admits to distrusting the offer of generous wages on the printed handbills; he recalls that when he was in gaol, he was told that wages in California were very low and that the workers lived in camps. Tom suggests that a lowering of expectation will reduce their disappointment if things do not turn out well. Reciprocating his gesture, Ma concludes that the handbills had cost someone a lot of money to print; would they have gone to such expense if there was no work to be had?

The Squatters' Circle

This is the first time that we see the circle, the formal gathering of the tenant farmer for 'figgerin''. As an exclusively paternalistic and hierarchical structure, Pa stands at the head, with the women and children standing to one side. In the context of the Joad family, where Ma is such a powerful figure, her exclusion from the process indicates that in this example at least, the circle is not what it should be. We also see that in the decision-making process, Tom Snr. lags behind his son; the decision to bring forward the time of departure, for instance, is down to Tom Jnr..[1]

Ma Joad and Symbolism

Whilst Ma is not officially part of the circle, her standing in the family demands acknowledgment. Steinbeck draws attention to this discrepancy with a symbolic demonstration. During the meeting, Ma makes two visits to the kitchen to perform culinary duties. In doing so, she handles objects made of iron and manipulates the flame of the stove. Iron, as the element which empowers man over nature, and fire, as the symbol of regeneration through destruction, is the preserve of those wielding power in the clan. Whilst her husband presides over the sham of a decision-making process, Ma says her piece in the language of earth magic.

The Nuclear Family and Collective Consciousness

With his observations of the Joad family in this chapter, Steinbeck begins to chart the development of a collective consciousness within the migrant community. When they abandon their farms, the small farmers leave behind the individualism of the middle class. As farmers, the extent of their collectivism was the nuclear family, a distinct unit with boundaries that were rigorously defended. When the Joads assemble in this chapter, they do so as in response to an audible call. As they set about their work they resemble the components of a machine, each member appearing to know, instinctively, what to do. There is no independent direction given to their activity, noone issues instructions, but from the outside it appears as if a single intelligence guides the process. This is what collective consciousness looks like in action.

The first rupture with the old ways occurs when Ma has to insist, to Pa's shame, that Casy be allowed to travel with the family. She

---

1   J. H. Timmermann, 'The Squatters' Circle in *The Grapes of Wrath*'; in *B. A* Heavilin, ed., *The Critical Response to John Steinbeck's 'The Grapes of Wrath'*. (London: Greenwood Press, 2000) 137–146, 137.

understands that exceptional circumstances demand exceptional solutions. In this instance, it is the family's boundary that stands in the way, and as with other obstacles to their progress, it must be removed. The nuclear family remains the building block of society, but on the road, the boundaries are fully permeable, facilitating the extension of the familial welcome to others in the same predicament. The open-handedness with which Ma welcomes Casy is a prominent feature of life on the road; that she understands this before they have even begun, is an early indication of the role that she is to play.

Rose of Sharon

In a book that gives so much to Feminism in its portrayal of Ma Joad, we should note that Rose of Sharon, a female barely out of childhood, pays a terrible price for having to leave her home. In this chapter, we detect a deterministic bent to the narrator's report. Her body and demeanour are but mirrors to maternity, her potential as a rational, capable being negated as pregnancy is all that would appear to matter about her.

Chapter 11

In a significant ecological statement, Steinbeck discusses the destructive potential of industrialism. He begins with the assertion that mechanization in agriculture is a paradox. In traditional farming, Nature and man create synergy, they amount to something much greater than the sum of their parts. A man who works the land with a team of horses understands this fact, he belongs. The man who drives a tractor, which may be left for months on end without attention, and who may live many miles away from his work, does not understand, he does not belong.

When humanity abandons a site, nature colonizes it. Nature's reclamation of dereliction may be so successful that, superficially at least, the illusion of human occupation may still be suspected.

Chapter 12

Route 66 is the main highway of the migration. A concrete river, its tributaries run in spate as the farmers are forced onto the road, resulting in a flood along its main course.

As well as hardship and uncertainty, the actual task of driving antiquated vehicles proved to be an ordeal of some magnitude for the migrants. Steinbeck draws attention here to the fine tolerances, close control and prolonged effort of concentration that driving clapped out automobiles demands.

To attempt this journey was to defy the odds. Pondering the question of faith, Steinbeck relates an anecdote from the lore of the migration of a man who towed a family all the way to California and fed them to boot.

A theme of *The Grapes* is the paucity of business morality amongst those who buy from and sell to the migrants. The salesman featured here is typical of Steinbeck's representation of such a person and we deduce, therefore, that on the road, business is theft.

Chapter 13

Through his descriptions of everyday occurrence, Steinbeck shows that for the Joads, the mundane has become extraordinary, and that they must adjust their thought and behaviour accordingly. At the gas station, Tom and Casy encounter mistrust from the established community. Tom is stung by the affront and reacts aggressively. Both he and Casy insist that their predicament is due to a failure of the system, not to any shortcomings on their part. Tom correctly predicts that the gas station owner is struggling financially, whilst Casy pushes the collectivist line, explaining that action by the many is required to defeat whatever it is that causes their hardship. They have begun to defend the migrant identity.

The Nuclear Family

The Wilsons may be minor characters but they embody the spirit of socialization that prevails on the road. It is their selfless hospitality which redeems the circumstances of Grampa's demise. Once again, the boundary of the nuclear family dissolves as the migrants extend familial rights in solidarity with those in need.

Grampa

Despite his bravado, Grampa was tied to his land every bit as much as was Muley Graves. When the time came, he was unable to make it out of his home state. The questions the family have to answer when burying him would have been inconceivable just a few days before. Their past life is now a distant memory, buried alongside Grampa.

Chapter 14

An intercalary in which Steinbeck warns the business community of the great error they make in mistaking effect for cause. The history of humanity has been one of progress, albeit with setbacks along the way. 'Manself' is distinguished by the preparedness to suffer and die for a concept. The banks and big growers risk the growth of a mass, collectivist movement with their policies. The description of the tractor ploughing the field offers a metaphorical comparison with the changes taking place within the minds of the people.

Chapter 15

An intercalary which, like Chapter Five, interrupts the flow of Free Indirect Style with the insertion of a conversation between characters. We suspect the break in format to imply special emphasis and as Steinbeck gives rein to his impressionistic gifts, we are not disappointed.

There is a contrast in this chapter between people who are prepared to empathize with those suffering misfortune, and those who are not. Al and Mae are unable to resist the migrants, and the truckers are unable to resist Al and Mae. The businessman and his wife, however, embody a type that Steinbeck identifies as being an aggravating factor in the humanitarian crisis of the migration. As people, they reassure themselves that 'business is noble and not the curious ritualized thievery they know it is';[1] Mae supplies comments on their activities, however, that suggest the contrary.

The conversation between the migrant father and Mae stands out for its poignancy. Unlike the banks and big land companies, whose decision-makers operate many miles from the site of wealth creation, Al and Mae are face-to-face with their clients. To spurn them is far more difficult than it is for the corporate boss, isolated in a remote office.

The automobile crash is a metaphor for the socio-economic disaster predicted in the previous chapter. It is a catastrophe that will affect all levels of society, not just the poor.

Chapter 16

Structurally, this chapter is significant as an example of Steinbeck's Dialogism, with successive set-piece situations giving new shape to the Joad legend. The mechanical breakdown foregrounds issues the family must settle if they are to survive. Ma Joad had intimated her misgivings previously and now is the time to act. In a roadside *coup d'état*, no less, she takes up the symbolic iron to claim ascendancy over the clan. A startling event in the lives of these conservative people, it is a statement from Steinbeck on the process of evolution, whereby the new direction is taken up from the wreckage of the old.

The Joads receive their first warning about California from the 'ragged man'. This pathetic figure embodies the fact that California is a hostile environment for migrant workers, surrendering knowledge that had cost him a wife and two children in its acquisition.

Al

The conversation between Al and Tom, as they drive into town, reveals the very great differences that exist between them. In withholding

---

1   Steinbeck, J., 2000. P161.

money from his father, Al has committed a grave offence against the family. Collective discipline is what gives the Joads the chance to survive and when he compounds the error by proposing that they spend the money on alcohol, we realise that Al has not yet reached the stage where he can accept adult responsibility. Throughout the book, we see that the Joad offspring remain as an appendage to their mother. Only Tom, whose enforced absence in gaol broke the dependency, is able to think with any amount of adult perspicacity.

Tom as Christ

Tom and Al meet the one-eyed man at the breaker's yard and in the spirit of socialization, Tom shows his preparedness to extend beyond the confines of his personal concerns to assist those less fortunate than himself. He also shows himself to be a shrewd judge of character. Penetrating the one-eyed man's sullenness, Tom sees the devastation his deformity has caused. He could have kept his counsel, leaving the man to continue his self-destructive course, but to have done so would have been an act of selfishness and against the code by which the migrants live. Tom is too good a man for that and with his compassion roused, risks his mission for a confrontation with the fellow over his self-indulgence and wastefulness. Critics have debated Steinbeck's representation of the Christ figure, and in this episode, Tom stakes his claim with a noteworthy display of selflessness and courage.

On arrival at the camp, Tom shows the difficulty he has in accommodating his take-it-as-it-comes philosophy in the new life. His disagreement with the proprietor, an incident which could have escalated beyond the point of reconciliation, confirms that Tom is overly sensitive to slights against his family. This is a dangerous weakness for Tom. As he leaves the camp, he shows that he has begun to unburden himself of the psychological baggage of prison. His admission to being 'bolshevisky' indicates a political awakening and marks the beginning of his education in the workers' struggle.

Chapter 17

An intercalary giving a broad sweep of the migrant experience. In a world that is constructed and dismantled on a daily basis, a new identity within the American people has been formed. There is a natural hierarchy determined by wisdom and expertise, and a code of conduct underpinned by consensus. Culturally, there is a sensitivity to genealogy, nostalgia and music, and the migrants retain a respectably bourgeois aspiration for their children.

Collective Consciousness

As we observed when the Joads prepared for the journey in Chapter Ten, the erection of the camp and the tasks of domestic life are carried out as if by a human machine. The individual dissolves into the family, and the family dissolves into the community of the camp. It is indicative of the mutual trust that bonds the community that there is a marked lack of self-consciousness amongst the residents.

Chapter 18

As a Dialogic novel, the emphasis on set-piece episodes results in an uneven spread to the transmission of information. Only that which feeds the author's intention has a place. For instance, Steinbeck deals with New Mexico, a state with no significance to the Joad narrative, in one short sentence.

As they near their destination, the Joads feel a corresponding increase in hostility. The conversation between the two boys at the gas station is typical of the local attitude. At the level of officialdom, the border guards encountered in Arizona, supposedly preventing the unregulated distribution of plants, are in effect outriders for the *Bum Blockade*, the shameful state policy of Depression-era California aimed at restricting the movement of migrant workers.

Another Warning

The menfolk receive their second warning from people returning from California whilst bathing in the river at Needles. They are told that although California is beautiful, the land is owned by a wealthy minority who do not permit others to grow crops, even in fields that have been left fallow. Also, the migrants, stigmatized as *Okies*, are feared by the locals and are not permitted to mix with them. Casy finds another piece of his jigsaw in this conversation. The man who owns a million acres but is unhappy and afraid to die, confirms to him that material accumulation is pursued merely as compensation for spiritual poverty.

Ma Joad

The events of this chapter provide a stern test for Ma Joad. When she refuses the Jehovite woman's offer of Grace for Granma, the woman and her friends go ahead anyway, but in their own tent. Granma appears soothed by the experience and Ma reflects on her decision. Has Casy and his ideas corrupted her judgment in matters of religion?

On being awoken by the deputy, Ma's defensive reflex is to defend herself with the iron skillet. She is taken aback by the hostility she faces simply because she has travelled from Oklahoma. As in the instance with the Jehovite woman, she does not yield and shows that, as the head of her family, she will not submit to intimidation.

When Granma does finally die, Ma understands that she cannot announce a fact that would jeopardize their mission. Bluffing her way through the inspection at Daggett, particularly given the extent to which she was herself fatigued, required great fortitude. When she does announce the death, however, it is Tom and Casy alone who fully appreciate the enormity of her effort.

When Ma and Pa compliment Tom on his growing maturity, Ma acknowledges her over-protectiveness. By this point the reader is well aware of this failing, which prevents her brood from developing into fully-formed adults.

Chapter 19

An intercalary that describes the historical process of agriculture in California as the taking of the land by men hardened by hunger from men softened by wealth. Steinbeck discusses the progression from small-scale farming to the large-scale manufacture of crops as a process of monopolization. As general businessmen, the growers pursued profit at the expense of the workers, who were forced to exist on subsistence-level wages.

If hunger was a determining factor, however, then it was the migrants who held the upper hand. Unlike the urban, middle class Californians, they were tormented by fields left barren for the artificial inflation of crop prices. Attempts to grow crops covertly on this land attracts what appears to be a disproportionately harsh response from the authorities. However, if the raising of a crop gives a man rights, gives him the justification to stand his ground and fight, then the sheriff's department were well advised to stamp it out. Compounding the reaction to the migrants was the generally held opinion that they were not really American. The conundrum for the great owners was that repression increased the threat of an uprising. They could not match the migrants' appetite, but what else could they do?

Chapter 20

Fresh from Granma's burial, the Joads arrive at *Hooverville*, a dirty and disorganised camp. Such places offered the sharpest expression of the migrant experience and the atmosphere of 'slovenly despair' which greets their arrival rapidly transforms into one of armed confrontation.

Steinbeck's dependence upon dialogue in lieu of an omniscient, third person narrator is eased with his use of characters who transmit generous amounts of information when they speak. In this chapter, the Joads meet Floyd Knowles, a seasoned camp dweller who opens their eyes to hitherto unforeseen aspects of the nightmare that is life on the road.

Police harassment is the first subject discussed. The notion that his people are not wanted in California is one that Tom is yet to fully grasp. He struggles to understand that the fear and prejudice of the Californians will sustain any level of persecution, regardless of how hard the migrants work.

Knowles then settles the issue of the handbills. He explains why many more workers are invited than are required. Tom's point about workers taking strike action at harvest time is a valid one, as that is when the growers are at their most vulnerable. Knowles, however, as the old hand, is able to counter. He explains that the authorities have realised that strikes require leaders and have become adept in the apprehension of anyone pretending to that role. Tom bridles against this and resolves to fight; the prospect of acquiescing is more than he can stomach. But Knowles counsels him again. Tom must know that if he resists the cops he will be beaten, and possibly fatally. Effective defence against a repressive regime requires discipline and organization, not hot-headedness.

Floyd Knowles and Steinbeck's Dialogism

Tom and Casy discern an ominous mood amongst the people in the Hooverville camp. Casy reckons that when he was a preacher he could calm disaffection with prayer, but in these circumstances, it would have had little effect. With the arrival of the contractor, the atmosphere in the camp becomes charged. Despite his counselling of Tom to the contrary, Floyd steps forward as the spokesman, recklessly taking the fight to the enemy. Why would he do this? The contractor, prepared for this eventuality, has Knowles pronounced a criminal on the spot. From this point onwards his struggle to find work will become harder, and the possibility that he will end his days murdered by fascists becomes all the more likely. This shows the helplessness of the individual when the time for their signature idea has come. Floyd Knowles abandons the discipline of fatherhood as the implacable resolve to fight exploitation takes possession of his being; an idea that made of him that most precious of resources in the migrant community: a leader of the struggle.

The Squatters' Circle

This episode also affords the opportunity to discuss the squatters' circle. Essentially a screen for the projection of masculine power, Ma's insurgency has, up until this point, restricted its influence within the Joad family. However, in this incident, we see that the circle is an organizational device that may take on special relevance at times of conflict. The organizing principle of the circle is rigid, hierarchical and gendered, but it has a flexible boundary which breaks down and forms again around new members. It is a type of direct democracy that in this instance takes on a mass character. When the contractor arrives, there is more than one circle to be seen. However, when he makes his announcement, the men congregate making a single 'compact group' near to his car. Three men speak to the contractor, but separately, and there is no interruption or disturbance from the others. The discipline of the circle holds, even when it encompasses the whole camp. When the leader steps forward, he does so with the force of numbers behind him, not as a lone voice.

The Joad Men

The incident also illuminates differences between the males in the Joad entourage. Casy and Tom show decisiveness in thought and action when under pressure. Effecting Knowles's escape was a great service to the camp and proved their commitment to the cause to all present. Pa and Uncle John, however, are found wanting. Life on the road has been particularly hard for them and we sense that they are becoming infantilized by their experience. For Pa there is a public rebuke from his wife for the insensitive manner in which he spoke about Connie; for John it is the ignominy of his having to be retrieved from a drunken stupor as the family faced crisis.

Ma Joad and Tom

One of Ma's main concerns for Tom is that his character has become tainted by experience. As they drive away from *Hooverville*, she

detects a belligerence in his tone. She reminds him of the story of
Pretty Boy Floyd, a fugitive criminal who was baited by the police
and died at their hands. Unlike Pa, who is swept along by events, Ma
has a very firm hold on what she prizes the most. The man that Tom
has become is foremost amongst her possessions and she will not
relinquish her grasp.

Having escaped the mob, Ma is required to bolster Tom's resolve.
She counters his exasperation by placing in context their present
suffering, explaining that the experience will make them stronger,
that they will endure where their persecutors will not. The potency
of Ma's argument was not lost on John Ford, the director of the film
version, who positioned the speech as the climax to his movie.

Symbolic Iron

When accosted by the cowards of the armed mob, Tom reaches for
the tyre lever to use as a weapon. He is restrained from doing so,
however, by his mother, and whilst we hear her plea for him not to
soil himself with violence, we also know that iron, as the symbol of
power, belongs to her: she is the leader and she alone may sanction
its use.

Chapter 21

An intercalary marking the change taking place in the lives of the
migrants, and the monopolization process in agriculture. The migrants
moved from being tied to forty acres to a fluid dispersal on the
promise of work. Castigated as *the other* they became a self-fulfilling
prophecy. Frightening men of property into a collective reflex,
armed groups were raised to fight them. The big growers boosted
their profits by lowering the rate of pay. They bought canneries and
sold crops at a price the small farmers could not match. Having been
forced onto the road, the small farmers' land was absorbed by the
combines. It was inevitable that the accumulation of bad experience
would weigh heavily on the migrants. Steinbeck's great fear was that
this widespread disaffection, if ignored, would serve as a fountain-

head for revolt. This is the point he makes with the title. The second line of the *Battle Hymn of the Republic*, 'He is trampling out the vintage where the grapes of wrath are stored', suggests a metaphor for the process and at this point in the book we feel its full force.

Chapter 22

Set in the Government camp at Weed, this chapter gives insight into the organization of the camp, and the allegorical connection to the flight of the Israelites. In the book of Exodus, the Ten Commandments were the new code by which the Israelites were to live; in the Government camp at Weed, the unemployed and itinerant labourers of California also learn a new way. In the teeth of a 'localized fascism', these people, under the umbrella of government protection, create a community dedicated to the common good. The camp is more than a place to live, it is a monument to the ability of ordinary people to organize a successful community with civilized values. Given the wider context of Depression-era America, it offers a political statement of some strength: a proletarian realization of the American Dream.

Tom's encounter with the Wallace family, where food and the work available to them is shared, is typical of the ethos of the camp. We learn that generosity is the basis of consensus and hoarding is forbidden. As people, they combine vigour with open-handedness in the knowledge that their basic needs will be met.

Ma Joad's meeting with the Ladies' Committee of Sanitary Unit Number Four is a deceptively presented visitation to issues of key importance in working class organization. Parodying the bureaucratic mind-set of the committee person, Steinbeck establishes a lightness of tone. However, when they meet Mrs Joyce, whose daughters have provoked consternation, the pomposity of their *bureaucratese* melts into a heartfelt espousal of the principles upon which the camp is based. From their comments, perhaps the following manifesto could be proclaimed for the camp:

- Poverty is not to be borne in private. It is a condition of residence that anyone with a need that the camp makes provision for must declare it.

- Pride is a sin and charity is forbidden.
- If someone has something to give it is donated to the camp for distribution.
- No person may set themselves above another as a benefactor.

Childhood

Throughout the book, Steinbeck casts light on the experience of children. At the croquet court, Ruthie disturbs play and drives the other children away. Her conduct is disturbing and raises the issue of childhood mental health in the migrant community. The response of the woman superintendent, calm and welcoming, provides reassurance that whilst in the camp at least, the children will be cared for.

Opposition to the Government Camp

The success of the camp is not to everyone's liking and in this chapter, Steinbeck discusses ways that opposition manifests itself. When Tom goes to work with the Wallace's, for instance, the farmer, Mr Thomas, tells them of the ultimatum he has been given by the Farmers' Association. The rate he has been paying his workers is considered too high and he must reduce it. The cut in pay will affect the workers' living standard; Wallace and his wife have an infant child and lower wages may force them to leave the camp. Another threat comes from the religious zealot, Lisbeth Sandry. Careful to select a naive and gullible target in Rose of Sharon, she instils terror with her talk of devil worship in the camp. To a vulnerable girl, the intensity with which she speaks gives plausibility to her message, a toxic threat to the trust that bonds the residents.

Jim Rawley

In light of the threat from the enemies of the camp, it is evident that the role of manager is both tremendously important and demanding. Jim Rawley is a man of considerable standing amongst the migrants and commentators have observed that his white clothes identify him as a Christ figure. He is certainly distinguished by great sensitivity as he deals with the camp-dwellers. Ma Joad admitted that she had been made to feel ashamed by her experience on the road, but following Rawley's visit her fears and suspicions were allayed. Likewise, when Rosasharn had been frightened by Lisbeth Sandry, Rawley assuages her fears. We note that even though he is fully supportive of Ma and Rosasharn, he does not condemn the other woman, asking instead that people be patient with her. So effective is Rawley's diplomacy that we detect a softening in Ma, a preparedness to trust, which had been shaken from her on the road.

Chapter 23

An intercalary that discusses the leisure activities of the migrant worker. We note again that migrant activity is distinguished by its social character; other than the man who shuns company to drink alone, everything mentioned has a distinct, communal character. From the culture of speech and jokes arose storytelling. In the examples given, a man relates his experience of fighting in the army against Native American people. The tale is relayed by the narrator in Free Indirect Style, the heart-breaking poignancy of its universalist theme enhanced by its being taken from first-hand experience.

Alongside storytelling, it is music that provides the most effective cultural expression. Using the instruments of the string band (harmonicas, fiddles and guitars), the performances may be organized or impromptu and draw appreciative crowds either way. Whilst there is acknowledgment of the technical aspects of musicianship, the real business is dance. As a courtship ritual played out in full view of the community, social dancing is integral to the cycle of renewal. The narrator gives voice to a woman's recollection of being led from the dancefloor to the fields by her beau. Her Cherokee father had thought to prevent them, but understood that in doing so, he would be acting against nature.

With the description of a Baptism, again, we see that the migrants behave collectively, not as private individuals. In a ceremony of great emotional and physical intensity, the preacher lifts people from the ground and pitches them into the water. The physicality of the descriptions are stark and have clear sexual connotations.

The folk basis of migrant culture is clear from the collective participation and barest minimum of paraphernalia required for its performance. It is organic and it is convenient. Most people contribute to the experience and there is no discernible division of labour between producer and consumer. The account given of the man who went to the cinema is an instance of migrants engaging with non-folk cultural forms. On his return, he talks to his friends who are inquisitive about the film. He attempts to summarize the story, but succeeds only in dumbfounding them. The apparent absurdity of the conversation, however, makes a very powerful comment about cultural production. What may appear to be stupidity is actually an expression of alienation. What is missing from the man's account of the film is the attempt to decode the metaphorical frame. Conventional readings of texts, as shaped by the big motors of cultural production, by class and race and gender, have appeal in proportion to the extent with which the reader may see at least part of their own life within them. For the migrants, cut adrift and reviled, the narratives of Hollywood meant very little.

Chapter 24

The Saturday evening dance is a showcase for the migrant world. There is a challenge from fascists, but the camp emerges in triumph.

Collective Consciousness

Steinbeck's impressionistic technique illuminates the account of the preparations for the Saturday evening dance. The sense of a common purpose is so strong that we are again able to make comparison with a human machine; individuals perform designated tasks seemingly unaware of the overall objective.

Threat of Attack

From the Central Committee discussion, we hear that outsiders have plotted to disrupt the dance. Impressively, the committee has a contingency for dealing with this eventuality, and if successful, will prevent the deputies, whom they have identified as instigators of trouble, from entering.

The dialogue in this passage imparts very useful contextual information to the reader. We learn that the growers dislike government camps because they raise the expectations of the migrants, making the prospect of disorder all the more likely when they stay in private camps with fewer facilities. They also believe that the migrants conceal agitators within their midst, and conspire to defraud the state of welfare payments. The memorable comment from one of the migrants that, "'This here's United States, not California'",[1] provides a succinct expression of their belief in Roosevelt's *New Deal*. Central government intervention was seen to be the solution to localized prejudice and discrimination. In the event, the camp defence operation is executed to perfection, providing a triumph for the migrants over the hated deputies.

Pa

At the 'figgerin'' circle, Pa gives the impression that he is a man who can make a tough decision and act upon it in the interest of his family. On closer scrutiny, however, it is the suspicion that he does not fully understand his predicament that prevails. The men discuss the auctioning of their work and see no end to the downward spiral in their rate of pay. Pa's comments about working for twenty cents an hour, getting some land and sending his children to school, understate the complexity of the issue and insult the other men, who all share the same aspirations. The advance in consciousness made by Tom at the *Hooverville*, and by Casy some time previously, is not yet in the offing for Pa.

---

1   Steinbeck, 2000, 349.

Chapter 25

An intercalary discussing the catastrophe in agriculture, with particular attention paid to the effect of the *Agricultural Adjustment Act (AAA)*. An often commented upon chapter, it is referred to as the *Jeremiad*, with Steinbeck's accumulated criticism of large scale agriculture likened to the lamentations of Jeremiah in the Bible.

The wonderfully evocative descriptions of a California landscape lush with produce are tempered with the knowledge that it is a thoroughly engineered environment, dedicated to profit. Steinbeck lavishes praise on specialists whose efforts have effected tremendous efficiency and fecundity in agriculture. However, in the present climate, the combined effects of monopolization and the *AAA* threaten not only to halt progress, but to actually turn the clock backwards.

He discusses the growth of large farms and of how the accumulation of land has become a compulsion for the wealthy. The big growers have learnt that when their poorer brethren are forced onto the road, the vacant land is theirs for the taking. To hasten the process, they set a price for the crop which the small farmer cannot match, thereby forcing them into debt.

Using Free Indirect Style, Steinbeck gives a voice to the small farmer. Given the reference to the *Battle Hymn of the Republic* in the title, we feel that we have arrived at the heart of the book when we read of the grape harvest in this chapter. Giving an account of the harvest, which could not be done properly without losing money, Steinbeck shows that one compromise may lead to another until there is nothing left of the original intention.

Across the state, the stench of decay from rotting food provides a metaphor for the crisis, yet worse is to come. The *AAA,* which ran from 1933–36, allowed for the destruction of crops deemed surplus to market requirements. As part of its commitment to the recovery of agriculture, the government guaranteed the price that farmers received for goods. In the event of the widespread availability of an item, which would normally have resulted in a reduction in price, the farmers were allowed to withhold as much of the crop as was needed to keep prices high. In a land where people literally starved to death, the consequences of the *AAA* were controversial to say the least, and given the professed intentions of the Roosevelt regime, a paradox of some magnitude.

Chapter 26

In an incident filled chapter, the Joads leave the *United States of America* for the hell that is California. Ma Joad is an irresistible force that brooks no dissent. She has given the menfolk ample opportunity to redeem themselves, but since the roadside *coup d'état*, she alone has the power to direct.

Ma leads her family in accordance with the accepted rules of hierarchy: she is not subversive. Having commented with sarcasm on the reversal of gender roles, Pa compounds his error with the suggestion that he may give his wife a beating. In her response, Ma makes it clear that lapses in propriety of this magnitude will not be tolerated. Taking Pa's comments literally, she trumpets his failings for all to hear, disregarding his sensitivity to public criticism, particularly in front of their children. Having uprooted her family from the comfort and security of the camp, she is out to prove her mettle as their leader.

Ma and Tom

In an audit of the forces at her disposal, she bemoans the failings of the family. However, for Tom, she is prepared to gamble her last dollar on a treat as they drive through Bakersfield. As Tom is the one person she can truly rely upon, she makes it plain that he is worthy of the outlay. She also exonerates him for striking the deputy, even though she counselled him previously against taking such action.

Evolution

There seems little enthusiasm within the family for what they are doing. Like children they reluctantly follow the parent figure, offering token resistance in the form of sullenness. Evolutionary development does not seem to embrace all members of the family equally. It is Ma, possessed of the idea that her family must be led to a new home and future, and Tom and Casy, who answer the appeal of the wider collective, who have made the leap; the others are drawn along like sheep.

Symbolism

On arrival at the camp at Pixley, Ma demonstrates again that she can manipulate symbolically important elements. This time it is fire, the force for renewal through destruction. With the fire she makes in the hut, she invokes powers that will cleanse her family now that they have found work.

Dialogism

As leader, Ma radiates the aura of authority. Whilst in the grocery store, she is drawn into a tense discussion with the storekeeper. Under the pressure of Dialogic exchange, Ma extracts an act of working class solidarity from the man, who is, to all intents and purposes, a company stooge. Once again, we see Steinbeck use the signature idea to reveal the fullest extent of a character's personality.

Rose of Sharon Joad

Impressive as she is, there is a question to be answered about Ma Joad with regard to her daughter. Throughout, Ma is consistently harsh on this young woman, whom, we suspect, is picking up the tab for her mother's feminist largesse. For a young woman who craves nourishment for the child in her womb, Rosasharn's protest is muted to say the least. Little more than a girl, she has suffered terribly since they left home. When she hysterically rounds on Tom, accusing him of a sinfulness that has brought punishment on her baby, it is the first time that she has given voice to her concerns with anything like the force they merited. The chastisement she receives after her outburst is typical of the oppression she suffers, and suggests that Ma has blinded herself to the specific needs of femininity as she forges ahead in her role as the head of the family.

With the gift of a pair of earrings, presumably in acknowledgment of Rosasharn's passage into womanhood, we detect cynicism. A gesture calculated to appease not celebrate, it was milk for her baby that she needed, not personal ornamentation. Indeed, it is a nagging concern that since the announcement in the Weed camp that Rosasharn was to have milk, she did not receive any. When Winfield is taken ill and given milk, we suspect dishonesty with regard to his sister. If it was so important, why was she overlooked? Has an unspoken decision been taken about the unborn baby? Perhaps Connie's abandonment of the family (and we note that Noah is never discussed after deciding to remain at the river) is a crime which condemns his unborn child?

Issues of Working Class Organization

In Tom's farewell conversation with Willie and Jule, the men discuss the camp in terms of the wider struggle against the bosses. Their conundrum, whether to stay in the camp and slowly starve through want of work, or leave and be persecuted by the authorities, shows their lives to be little more than a choice between different kinds of confinement. Willie introduces the subject of working class solidarity and strikes. He cites the unity of the migrants as the reason why the deputies have not attacked the camp. If they did enter, they would instantly be faced with a force several hundred strong. Jule raises the issue of leadership. Expressing the same sentiment as Floyd Knowles at the *Hooverville* camp, he identifies the need for leaders as an intrinsic weakness in the strike tactic. When the bosses identify the leaders, they simply have to pick them off and the movement is halted.

The Hooper Ranch, Pixley

The Joads enter the Hooper Ranch oblivious to the fact that a strike is in progress. Only Tom, despite the poor accommodation and forced labour conditions, is sufficiently curious as to the disturbance at the gate to investigate further. Pa and Uncle John, like children, have no interest beyond the family hearth. Tom's resolve is such, however, that not only is he able to find out the nature of the trouble, but he absconds from the camp and meets the striking workers. This is Tom's first involvement with a strike and he takes it upon himself to drum up support on their behalf.

The arrival of Casy and the imminent arrival of Tom in the labour union provides a clarification of purpose. It is the culmination of Casy's often cryptic musings and Tom's instinctual behaviour.

Casy as a Union Activist

Casy has completed his metamorphosis and is now a fully-fledged union activist. Whilst in gaol, he experienced an epiphany of the potential power of the masses during a dispute. The prisoners won concessions from the authorities by raising their voices together in protest. Casy discusses his new role, particularly the difficulty he has in persuading people to take action. He consoles himself with thoughts of a man he met in gaol who described the compulsion to act against oppression, regardless of the odds. It is to be understood that there will be losses as well as gains, but the struggle must go on.

Casy as Christ

The deputies raid the camp and surround the pickets. Casy's initials, JC, give a clue as to his identification as the Christ figure in this episode. Firstly, he is called 'That shiny bastard' by a deputy, indicating a luminous quality to his appearance. Secondly, he twice tells the deputies that they do not know what they are doing, which is, of course, a reference to Christ's words at Golgotha. Tom secures instantaneous, summary, retributive justice for his friend, then goes on the run.

Tom is now a Wanted Man

On his return from the fields, Pa reports on the events of the day. The anticipated drop in pay materialized and resulted in friction between the pickers which escalated to violence. Surprisingly—this is the first time that he has shown any sign of a proletarian class consciousness—Pa challenged the checkers, pointing out that they would not find anyone to work for that rate of pay. The big news of the day, however, is that the deputy struck by Tom has died and that he is now the subject of a manhunt. The deputies had fabricated a story that timed the death of the officer prior to that of Casy's, and a corps of reactionaries has been raised to deal with the matter by force.

Childhood

The children were exhausted by the work, which went unnoticed by Pa, whose only concern seems to be that they lack discipline. They do not look forward to going to school and Winfield is aware that migrant children are victimized. As the chapter draws to a close, the Joads have found a cotton ranch to work and Tom is in hiding.

Chapter 27

This intercalary offers a Dialogic pastiche in FIS which relates the thoughts of a cotton picker, which could be Pa, and two other voices, one of whom is a farmer.

Chapter 28

After the government camp, the boxcar camp provides the best accommodation the Joads have found. They establish the semblance of a domestic routine and even take a trip into town on a Saturday morning to purchase a new stove and clothing. The daily rhythm of camp life comes to an abrupt end, however, when Ruthie betrays Tom.

Ma as Leader

Ma again meets the challenge as the family's leader. She formulates a plan on the hoof and has the presence of mind to forbid Pa from mentioning to Ruthie the error she has made. As the leader it is she, unless she chooses to delegate the task, whom the accused must face. When Ruthie arrives it is plain that this tearful and embattled youngster did not intend to betray her family. Ma shows sensitivity to the fact with her gentle words of encouragement. Tom had commented on the need for the children to grow up, but it could not have happened overnight.

Ma has not seen Tom since they arrived, but she must warn him that he is compromised. As she makes her way to the hideout, we see that she is not a woman who is lost when away from home or the grocery store. She moves with the stealth of a huntsman *brave* and on reaching her destination conceals herself so well that the wildlife disturbed by her approach returns as she waits.

Natural History

Steinbeck's writing betrays here once more a keen interest in the natural environment. With brief, innocuous-sounding sentences such as 'The wind blew past and left the thicket quiet, but the rushing of the trees went on down the stream',[1] we again detect first-hand observation, Steinbeck's guarantee of faithful representation.

Ma and Tom

Ma and Tom agree that he must go away, but Ma does not want him to go too far. Tom discloses the change in his outlook. He has thought long and hard about Casy and has resolved to tread the same path. He sees the need to involve himself with his people in their struggle against injustice.

Losing Tom is a severe blow to Ma, but she must not allow her anguish to show. In an exemplary display of self control she negotiates

1   Steinbeck, 2000, 435.

not only an offer of work for her family whilst walking home, but also Al's courtship with their neighbours' daughter. Ma was able to calm the other family's concerns, and her husband's wounded pride, all at a time when she was coming to terms with the loss of her eldest son and chief ally.

Evolution

Pa's despair, and a fixation with nostalgia which drains him of effectiveness, are addressed by Ma when she suggests that women are better able than men to adapt to change. She reckons that if they can survive the ordeal of the road, they can survive anything. The weak have been lost, but those who remain grow stronger. However, on the following day, as the family readied themselves for work at the new ranch, we again observe conduct that undermines Ma's evolutionary claims. Al grumbles because he must get up, Pa complains of tiredness, and Rosasharn defies her mother's advice and insists on being allowed to work, despite her condition. Far too many workers turn up for the amount of work to be done and the job is finished before lunchtime. Rosasharn seems to have fallen ill and it begins to rain, a sign that the work of the harvest will soon be at an end.

Chapter 29

An intercalary describing the catastrophic flood which is likened to that of the book of Genesis in the Old Testament. The rainfall is prolonged and has a dramatic effect on the landscape. The migrants, now without work and desperate, succumb to begging and theft. In town, pity turns to anger and distrust. They are seen as a menace that must be controlled, and the apparatus for policing them is boosted. However, when the rain stops the men turn out for their 'figgerin'' circles as usual. Their anger, as it did in the opening chapter, confirms to the women that they are not yet beaten. It is noted that green shoots of new growth have appeared on the hillside, a sign of renewal and hope for the future.

Chapter 30

The final chapter and the point of severance in Steinbeck's chronicle of the Joad family. The migrants are divided as to whether they should stay or leave. Rosasharn has a fever, and Pa, rejuvenated in the absence of Tom, suggests the building of a dyke to prevent the flooding of the carriage. Whilst Pa's enthusiasm is not reciprocated initially, the help he needs is provided when Rosasharn goes into labour.

When Pa begins to dig the other men join him. They become absorbed in the task, which results in a 'fury of work, a fury of battle'. Pa has worked out that with the bank dug, the flood water will run into the field on the other side of the river. The plan fails, however, when a tree tears a hole in the bank. As the other men flee, Pa flings himself into the breach, Uncle John collapses in the stream, and Al, showing presence of mind, races to the car to start the engine before it is flooded, but all are thwarted.

The stillbirth of Rosasharn's baby provides an unsettling sense of anti-climax. This is one occasion where their straitened circumstances are a blessing, preventing the Joads from dwelling on the tragedy of their loss.

Matriarchy

The conversation between Ma Joad and Mrs Wainwright, in which they discuss the changes taking place in their lives, feeds into the general understanding that the migrants evolved as a community by adopting a socialized approach to the issues of day-to-day living. However, when Mrs Wainwright instructs the men to bury the infant's corpse, we note another aspect of their evolutionary development. In deflecting objections regarding legality, Mrs Wainwright shows that she, like Ma Joad, places the welfare of her family before any obligation to society. Like Ma, Mrs Wainwright is the head of her family, showing that an evolution which is matriarchal is not unique to the Joads.

Uncle John is tasked with the burial, but leaves the body in a box in the river instead. There is a comparison here with the infant Moses in Exodus. That Moses was the great prophet of the Israelites gives substance to Uncle John's wish for the baby's remains to act as a message to the people of the town.

Ma's explanation to Rosasharn about her baby elicits an act of fierce loyalty from the girl, who struggles to an upright position to exonerate her mother. There is a brief, inaudible conference between the two, which precipitates their immediate departure. Ma adopts a peremptory tone as she directs the evacuation, telling Pa to 'Git your back bent' at one point. As the family walk along the highway, the reason for the sudden evacuation becomes clear: Rosasharn is unwell.

Childhood

The children provide an interlude from the crisis with their squabble about a flower. The Joad children are not burdened with the concerns of adulthood, but on entering the barn they encounter a boy for whom childhood has become little more than a memory. In contrast to the carefree Joad children, this boy carries the burden of a provider. He is a junior member of the adult world, a man-boy, who stands as the antithesis of the boy-men of the Joad family. The boy has been given, or has assumed for himself, patriarchal authority, a reverse of the experience of Pa and Uncle John.

The Ending

The final action of the novel, which was suggested by the whispered conference between Ma and Rosasharn in the boxcar, has provoked much comment. The image of the adult male nursing at a woman's breast has its literary precedents, the short story *Idylle* by Guy de Maupassant being the most frequently cited. As in *Of Mice*, Steinbeck brings the book to a close with a scene which, far from tying up loose ends to offer a sense of benign closure, dramatically reopens the wounds his narrative inflicted to the social, economic and gender structures of hegemony.

The ending provides the sharpest expression of the warning issued by Steinbeck with this novel: that the abuse of the migrant people will cause great problems and may ultimately undermine the way of life for the whole of the country. Steinbeck was not a revolutionary. If he were, he would not have taken the trouble to warn the existing order of the error in their ways. His response is that of the patriot, the man who honours his commitment to a Constitution which requires that all Americans be treated equally before the Law.

At its conclusion, the novel suggests that matriarchy represents continuity. Ma Joad understands her experience to be extraordinary. In the mission to save her family, she will engage with, and consent to, whatever is necessary to see them through to better times. The young woman nurses the adult male to prolong his life, affirming Ma's comments on survival. However, it should also be noted that this image also has connotations for men such as Tom Snr. and John. Displaced from their positions they stand to one side like children at the 'figgerin'' circle. Dependant on the mother figure they have been infantilized, and the image of the suckling male offers an analogy of some graphic force for their position. With regards to circularity, the assumption that more propitious circumstances will see a return to patriarchy is open to conjecture. The prospect of Ma Joad and Mrs Wainwright timidly ceding control to men who have failed does not seem credible. The ascendancy of the women is a product of the struggle against adversity on the road; it is an organic development which prompted comparison with an evolutionary leap. Such gains are not surrendered lightly, and even if the Joads do find fortune, we cannot envisage anyone other than Ma to be at their head.

5. Critical Reception

5.1 Of Mice and Men

Whilst *Of Mice* was received with warmth by the critics, a stock reading of the text came into circulation that did little to encourage its further exploration. That Steinbeck's novella is a parable of pessimism, a testimony to the inescapable arbitrariness of life where, regardless of the care and thought expended, no plan may ever come to fruition, whilst valid as a reading, leaves a good deal more that can be said.

'The Dream of Independence': Joseph Fontenrose

Joseph Fontenrose (in Jill Karson ed. 1998) challenged received opinion with his contribution. Pointing out anomalies in the textual justification for the handed-down reading, Fontenrose saw a decoy that diverts attention from another thread of meaning.

He identifies two areas of weakness in the conventional reading: Steinbeck's use of the Robert Burns poem *To a Mouse*; and the incongruity, as he saw it, of Lennie and George's narrative. He suggests that the line from Burns referred to in the title, 'The best laid schemes o mice and men / Gang aft agley' does not dismiss all plans by all men, but merely some of them. He argues that the blanket interpretation derives from the sense of hopelessness that prevails amongst the ranch hands. Rhetorically, this places the cart before the horse, so to speak, with the coefficient interpreted in light of the text, rather than the other way around. Of George and Lennie's story, he observes that it certainly wasn't easy for bindlestiffs to buy their own farm, but neither was it impossible. He also suggests that the characters of Lennie and George do not possess the necessary gravitas to support the universalist message attributed to the story, which implies, of course, a serious error on the part of Steinbeck.

Through the mist of the deterministic theme, Fontenrose picked out another. George and Lennie's plan failed because it did not cater for pleasure seeking, an aspect of life so important that arrangements made without it are doomed to fail. Alongside the dream he shares with Lennie, George also harbours a yearning for sensual pleasure which he denies himself in the care of his friend. Fontenrose identifies George's inner psychological struggle to be the strongest aspect of the text, the drama of the conclusion springing from the choice he makes between conflicting dreams.

'Control and Freedom': Samuel I. Bellman

Samuel I. Bellman (also in Jill Karson) offers a Freudian reading of the text, with George and Lennie as symbolic figures, playing out the ego's struggle to control the id. Where George is the ego (the self or 'I' which perceives the external world and from which the 'I' response originates), Lennie is the id (all of the instinct and psychic quality that we are born with. Operating exclusively on the pleasure/pain principle it generates the energy for mental life and is not affected by the external world or the passage of time).

As Bellman points out, however, George is not fixed in the role of the ego and, leading up to the murder, he shows his liking for the desires and pleasures associated with the id. As the id figure, he becomes susceptible to control by his ego counterpart, and sure enough, at the novel's conclusion, George is led away by Slim, the leading hand at the ranch.

'The War Between Good and Evil': Leo Gurko

Leo Gurko (also in Jill Karson) reads *Of Mice* as an allegory of Manichean mythology's struggle between darkness and light.

Manicheism (or Manichaeism)

A religion founded in the 3rd Century by the Persian, Mani, it spread from Mesopotamia and Babylonia to Spain, France and Northern Italy. It has a central myth which goes through three distinct phases. In the first phase, light (or spirit, or God) became separated from darkness (or matter, or the Devil). This is followed by a period which includes the present time, where the two extremes encounter, mix and struggle with one another. The final stage, projected for the future, features another separation of the opposing forces. For the individual, one's fate at death is determined by the way one has led one's life; the righteous person enters paradise, whilst the fornicator, the materialist, the drunkard etc. is condemned to an endless cycle of reincarnation. Distinguishing Manicheism from other monotheistic religions is the belief that God and Satan are evenly matched, and it is possible that evil will be victorious. Gurko argues that this final point makes the myth a very attractive structural device for writers of fiction and drama.

With regard to *Of Mice*, Gurko identifies the central theme to be the struggle between Lennie and George, as representatives of good and evil, standing either side of the Manichean divide. He cites the exaggerated disparities in physical stature and personality, and the types of character whom they are drawn to, and repelled by, as evidence for his interpretation. Lennie, whose behaviour is driven by an unrestrained sensuality, stands for darkness. George, as the embodiment of light, is conspicuous for the care and intelligence attributed to his activity. Emphasizing the sense of illumination is the fact that his appearance is always described in detail. Gurko identifies two other characters who take part in the struggle: Curley's wife, who, as an unregulated sexual force, belongs to darkness; and Slim, the widely revered worker-aristocrat, whose dexterity and elegance position him, with George, in the light.

On the question of style, Gurko points out that Steinbeck generates a sense of antiquity with which to accommodate his mythological theme. Unlike the Victorian novel, say, with its emphasis on the nuances of character and the psychological insight afforded by the omniscient narrator, key aspects of *Of Mice* locate it more comfortably within the Epic tradition. In particular, it is the reciting by George of the shared dream of a farm, an act that he repeats at different times but always in the same manner and with the hint of rapture in both speaker and listener, that is suggestive of the refrain, a feature of the Epic.

'Misogyny in Of Mice and Men*'*

In an appropriately muscular feminist reading, in Jill Karson's collection, Jean Emery raps the knuckles of the Academy and its wider circle of literary reviewers, for privileging a sentimental, economic reading of the book at the expense of its more radical interpretations. She finds Steinbeck's fictional world to comprise of little more than a matrix of patriarchal power relations, a domain where hostility to women provides a lethal threat to femininity. She also discerns a dream at work which differs radically from that of the much circulated reading of the outlawed friendship struggling against impossible odds. She sees *Of Mice* as the fulfilment of patriarchy's fantasy of the elimination of women and femininity. She discusses George and Lennie as representative figures for masculinity and femininity respectively, and their relationship as a marriage. She identifies a generalized, though clearly defined struggle between the masculine and the feminine, and that masculinity has strategies, and as the dominant force a coercive apparatus, with which it maintains its position.

By focusing on George and Lennie as emblems of gender, we find her observations to ring true with the general pattern of the text. For all the advantages of his position as patriarchal lord and husband, George is dogged with insecurity. His diminutive physique makes it all the more difficult for him to appear convincing, particularly given Lennie's size and great physical strength. His unease is particularly conspicuous when he encounters women. Lennie, on the other hand, is portrayed as little more than an emotional force. He is directed by desires that he cannot rationalize; his femininity defined by docility, submissiveness and the need for reassurance. Emery adds that his desire to pet small animals indicates a maternal craving, and that his learning disability provides a crude comparison with the cliché of female intelligence perpetuated by patriarchy. She defines their marriage as stereotypical, with one as husband and the other as wife, and identifies the refrain, where George repeats for Lennie the details of their shared dream, to be their marital vow.

Emery discusses the paternalistic fear that women are a threat to masculine capability, and a collective consciousness amongst males that bolsters their resistance to feminine appeal. Of particular relevance here is Lennie's immense physical strength. As a feminine figure, his power increases the anxiety of the males and their estimation of a feminine force that endangers them. The ranch is a segregated environment which isolates women, and in acknowledgment of the importance attached to the display of control and mastery by the male, those men who, for whatever reason, are not able to fulfil their duties.

Cain and Abel (Genesis IV)

A significant proportion of critical comment on *Of Mice* concerns its allegorical connection to the Old Testament story of Cain and Abel. Steinbeck gives an utterly contemporary feel to the story, which serves as the beating heart of his social narrative of pre-Depression era America.

Cain and Abel were the sons of Adam and Eve; Cain tilled the earth and Abel tended sheep. The brothers brought offerings to God, who expressed appreciation to Abel but not to Cain. This angered Cain, whose displeasure was plain to see. God addressed Cain and chastised him for his anger. God instructed Cain to live righteously and to master the temptation of sin, lest he became prey to it. The brothers went to the fields and Cain murdered Abel. When asked by God as to the whereabouts of his brother, Cain replied with impudence, 'Am I my brother's keeper?' God cursed Cain, condemning him to the life of a fugitive, forbidding that he ever harvest the earth upon which his brother's blood had been spilt. Cain spoke again, pleading that the punishment was too great for him to bear; he feared reprisals and he feared for his life. God assured Cain that anyone who took his life would suffer a vengeance seven times greater than the punishment he had received, and placed a mark upon him that all who approached would know him.

'A Parable of the Curse of Cain': William Goldhurst

William Goldhurst's essay in Jill Karson's collection confirms with some force the allegorical connection between *Of Mice* and Genesis (IV), sketching out a dialogue between the texts that breathes the life of the twentieth century into the post-lapsarian parable. With echoes of Samuel Bellman's interpretation, he reads into the Cain and Abel story the struggle between ego and id, with the resolution of the allegory, the attempt to evade God's curse upon Cain, dependant on the outcome of the Freudian conflict, with Lennie and George doubling up in the lead roles.

Given the mistrust at the ranch for men who travel together, we must assume that in this place, Cain's question to the Lord, 'am I my brother's keeper?' will be answered in the negative. God's curse of Cain translates as the rootless, itinerant existence of the bindlestiffs, compelled to farm land but never to profit from the harvest. Cain's fear of God's punishment is attributed to a fear of solitude, the corrosive effects of which provide a palpable and far reaching undercurrent in the novel.

Goldhurst plots a see-sawing in the level of optimism for George and Lennie's scheme. Reaching a peak when Candy and Crooks buy in, it falters when Curley's wife attacks Crooks, the point at which God could no longer be answered, 'Yes, I am my brother's keeper'. The speech given by George after Curley's wife's body has been discovered, in which he dismisses the dream as a folly, returns him to the lonely existence of the curse of Cain. This is the point at which the full extent of the disaster is revealed, a blow which, for Goldhurst, provides the true climax of the novel.

Goldhurst discusses at some length the emblematic struggle between the rational mind and the appetites, as acted out by George and Lennie. He points out that the bindlestiff's routine visit to the *cathouse* served as a compromise solution, a fudge that allowed commerce and society to continue, whereas the attempt to subjugate the appetites completely, as symbolized by George's repeated attempts to impress upon Lennie the need for restraint, led to catastrophe.

'The Need for Commitment': Louis Owens

Like Joseph Fontenrose, Louis Owens in Jill Karson's collection, addresses the widely accepted view that *Of Mice* is a pessimistic tale that condemns the aspirations of man to failure. Unlike Fontenrose, however, Owens sees a redeeming feature in Steinbeck's foregrounding of commitment as a heroic characteristic.

He discusses Steinbeck's treatment of loneliness, the perceived prompt for Cain's questioning of God's judgment. Referring to Steinbeck's own comment, that Lennie represents the 'inarticulate and powerful yearning of all men', Owens suggests that his desire for soft, warm things to caress translates to a need for friendly contact with others. It is the same yearning that draws George to Lennie as much as Lennie to George, and why Curley's wife spends so much of her time wandering the ranch in search of company.

It is the novel's ending, however, that draws Owens's most telling comment. He sees the murder as a supreme act of loyalty, with George, assuming full responsibility for his friend, elevated to the position of hero. When he walks away with Slim at the finale, a note of triumph is discernible. Despite Lennie's death, the dream of mutual support survives and with it the hope of liberation from the curse of Cain.

Marilyn Chandler McEntyre on Cain, Abel and Innocence

In a bold and at times controversial reading of the book (in *John Steinbeck's 'Of Mice and Men'*, ed. Harold Bloom, 2006), M. C. McEntyre discusses the extent to which Steinbeck rehabilitates the moral message of the Old Testament story in *Of Mice*, and its reception by the reader today.

At the centre of the analysis is a perceived sleight of hand that

Steinbeck performs in his casting of a person with a severe learning disability in the role of Abel. Cain's question to God, 'Am I my brother's keeper?' may now be heard not as a hubristic riposte but the appeal of one exasperated with the care of a dependant sibling. The Biblical Abel is an innocent, but he has the wherewithal to tend a flock of sheep. In *Of Mice*, Lennie is also innocent because of his disability, but unlike his counterpart, he is completely reliant. This simple alteration to the equation throws the story open to interpretations far more sympathetic to the Cain figure. We also note that the Bible does not elaborate beyond the assertion that Abel is an innocent; in this text, Lennie shows cunning, and plays George like a wilful child throughout. For M. C. McEntyre, the question posed by Steinbeck is whether those who engage fully with the world are morally obliged to shoulder the burden of those who cannot. She asks whether innocence is compatible with adulthood and whether growing up necessarily involves guilt. For her, the modern reader is repulsed by Abel's childlike innocence, which makes their sympathy for him all the more unlikely.

Like Louis Owens, M. C. McEntyre sees Lennie's murder as a paradox that can be interpreted as an existential triumph. However, the telling point that she makes about Cain is that he is a symbol of modern America. Referring to capitalism and imperialism, she suggests that the emphasis of contemporary American society makes it very difficult for Americans to condemn Steinbeck's Cain with any real conviction.

5.2 The Grapes of Wrath

As a totem for the struggle against oppression, *The Grapes* divided critics into those who sympathized with the migrants and those who did not. The contributions considered here show the scope for interpretation when the narrowness of tribal conflict is set to one side.

'The Darwinian Grapes of Wrath*'*: Brian Railsback[1]

For Brian Railsback, *The Grapes* provides a clear and unequivocal affirmation of Charles Darwin's theory of evolution as applied to humanity in North America in the early twentieth century. In short, he compares Steinbeck's migrants with a species that is forced from its customary habitat which, in seeking a new home, struggles with adversity and loses many of its number in the process. The survivors, having shown remarkable resilience and adaptability, appear as a brand new species. The native population, alarmed by the strength of their new neighbours, contrives by whatever means at their disposal to expel them.

There is also acknowledgment of the hostility directed toward Darwin from the Church of the day. Steinbeck's unsympathetic portrayal of people of faith, with Casy's sexual misdemeanours and the attention drawn to the strange noises made by the Jehovites whilst praying, provide a fair indication of where his sympathies lie.

Railsback also notes that a Darwinian reading uncovers a rich seam of otherwise unhewn paradox in the text. He identifies two prominent examples brought to light by his analysis: that the exploitative practices of the bosses create a stronger foe than they have yet to face (through selection, only the fittest survive); and that the truly awful conditions endured by the migrants make them a more compassionate people. He also discusses the seemingly inexplicable sense of victory experienced by Ma and Tom amid scenes of abject poverty and alienation. He explains that in surviving ordeals engineered against them, they had passed the test of natural selection, and were, therefore, entitled to celebrate.

The Postmodern Novel (as discussed by Brian McHale, 1987)

A pressing concern of the Postmodern novel is the reliability of texts, and specifically, the compromise of ontological integrity due to the contamination of one ontological frame (mythological, fictional,

---

1   In Barbara A. Heavilin, ed., *The Critical Response to John Steinbeck's 'The Grapes of Wrath' 1938–41* (New York: Penguin, 1989).

historical etc.) by another. When the boundaries between frames are breached (Framebreaking), the reader is faced with an interpretative conundrum. When a text is read as a history, for instance, the reader will have certain expectations as to what a historical text is and what it does. If the writer introduces the suggestion of myth into the work, say, or the guest appearance of fictional characters, the value of the piece as a history will be diminished. In Chapter 4, for instance, the appearance of the land turtle in the Joad narrative presents the reader with just such a problem. In the intercalary that precedes, the turtle was offered as a symbol of the migration, but if it may suddenly appear in the fictional narrative of the Joads, it loses its symbolic value. Likewise, if Tom Joad may simply sweep up the symbol of migration as he walks along, he will transcend the fictional and enter the realm of the symbolic. The flattening of the boundary between the symbolic and fictional gives a duality to the text which, whilst expanding interpretative possibilities, also increases awareness of the extent to which all discourse is compromised.

'*A Postmodern Steinbeck, or Rose of Sharon Meets Oedipa Maas*': *Chris Kocela*

In his paper of this title, Chris Kocela refers to *The Grapes* as 'a postmodern novel long before it was fashionable to be so'.[1] Focusing his analysis on the contemporary historical and Biblical ontological frames, he finds much to support a Postmodernist reading. Contemporary history, the staple of the intercalary chapters, derives authority from fact and objectivity. The Biblical world, which arises from the allegorical comparison between the migrant workers of California and the Israelites of Exodus, assumes the timeless and symbolic qualities of the religious text. That there are sharp differences between the two is clear and we understand that any cross contamination would spoil both. For the historical narrative, it is the integrity of a discourse grounded in the empirical that would be lost.

---

1   C. Kocela, 'A Postmodern Steinbeck, or Rose of Sharon Meets Oedipa Maas', in Heavilin (2000), 249.

For the Biblical allegory, it is the authority to adjudicate, the privilege exercised by religious texts over other texts.

The evidence of contamination or compromise is evident in *The Grapes* from the very first paragraph. The historical event of the desertification of Oklahoma is described with a mixture of empiricism and cranked up, Bible sourced rhetoric, which instantly presents us with a conflict between two discourses. As the novel progresses, the alternation between worlds in the same narrative plane results in an oscillation of images, a series of confrontations that force the reader to continually scrutinize, paying particular attention to the boundaries that separate them.

'Dialogic Structure and Levels of Discourse in Steinbeck's **The Grapes of Wrath'***: Louis Owens and Hector Torrez* [1]

A pioneering theorist of the Dialogic novel was the Soviet Academic, Mikhail Bakhtin. Owens and Torrez discuss *The Grapes* in the light of his observations.

For Bakhtin, the novel was the quintessential literary form of the modern world. A *catcher's-mitt* for language and voice, its focus is the immediate present. Bakhtin divides the novel into two types, the Monologic (single voiced) and the Dialogic (multi voiced or polyphonic). The Monologic he describes as 'a multitude of characters and fates in a single objective world, illuminated by a single authorial consciousness'. The Dialogic, 'a plurality of consciousnesses, with equal rights and each with its own world, [which] combine but are not merged in the unity of the event'.[2] The Monologic novel, as exemplified by the confident Realism of the Victorians, faithfully portrays societal structure. Psychological transparency is achieved through the omniscient, third person narrator, the voice of authorial opinion that crowns the discursive hierarchy of the text. The Dialogic novel, by contrast, offers a less assured reading experience. The authorial voice, stripped of its privileges to intrude, describe and

---

1   In Barbara A. Heavilin ed. 2000.
2   M. Bakhtin, in C. Emerson, ed., *Problems of Dostoevsky's Poetics* (Minneapolis: University of Minneapolis Press, 1986), 6.

adjudicate, appears as one among many, and characterization becomes an exercise in the artistic portrayal of consciousness independent to that of the author.

The Grapes is a sumptuously Dialogic novel and in this study, Owens and Torrez attempt to apprehend Steinbeck's techniques for its achievement. They concern themselves primarily with the means by which the text resists closure and how Steinbeck achieves multi-voicedness. Resistance to closure, or to never having said the final word, is a key characteristic of the Dialogic novel. The sensitivity and receptiveness to the present makes it a ready vehicle for the next incident, at the moment of its occurrence.

The ending of *The Grapes* provides a clear example of how the Dialogic novel differs from the Monologic. The uncertainty as to what is being said, the sense that much more is about to occur and indeed should occur, given the predicament of the Joads, stimulates a sense of open-endedness. Certainly, as Owens and Torrez point out, the description in the preceding chapter of the green shoots of new growth that appear after the flood indicates a new beginning rather than an ending. Also, they argue that in a text so consistently Dialogic, so resistant to closure, why would the reader expect a climax, a reassurance, a tidying up of loose ends that the conclusion to the Monologic novel invariably provides?

In common with the Dialogic novel discussed by Bakhtin, *The Grapes* has no omniscient, third person narrator. But as Owens and Torrez point out, the intercalary chapters that serve as a substitute also contribute to the Dialogic quality of the text. The epic voice in the intercalaries is subject to dialogue with others, a pressure that effectively excises its ascendancy. Owens and Torrez single out Chapter Twenty-Five for specific analysis, where different narrator voices are brought together.

'The Grapes of Wrath': Joseph Fontenrose

WWithin the wide ranging discussion included in Barbara A. Heavilin's book (2000), Joseph Fontenrose, with reference to the work of Peter Lisca, leaves little doubt as to the connectedness of

Steinbeck's novel to the Bible. Having outlined the main points of the dominant allegory (the flight of the Israelites) in the Introduction, I focus here on Fontenrose's supplementary observations.

The book of Exodus is, understandably, referenced extensively in connecting the Joad narrative with the flight of the Israelites. But from other details in the book, it is clear that Steinbeck connects the migrants to the Israelites in a wider sense as well. The story of the infant Moses for instance, is clearly discernible in the manner in which John Joad disposes of the remains of Rosasharn's stillborn baby in the final chapter. Likewise, when Steinbeck makes clear the preference of the migrants for monogamy, we see common ground between them and the Israelites (Exodus 22:16). The meeting of God and Moses on Mount Horeb (Exodus 3:1 and 17:6), whilst part of the flight narrative, also provides a plausible analogy for the time that Jim Casy spent in the hills, wrestling with the dilemma of a loss of faith. Casy's story also connects with the Temptation of Christ in the Gospels (Matthew 4:3-4; and Luke 4:1-13). The struggle between good and evil, between God and the Devil, for possession of the soul, is a precursor to the preacher's return. Indeed, the presence of a Christ figure is one of the more obvious connections between The Grapes and the New Testament. Whilst it has been argued that it is Jim Rawley, the leader of the migrants in the Government camp, Fontenrose's preferred candidates are Jim Casy and Tom Joad. He sees Casy, a self-sacrificing figure who understands the power of human communion, to be the antithesis of the traditional Christian John Joad, a man paralysed by guilt and doubt. For Tom, he refers to Ma Joad's belief in him and his difference from the others. Other similarities include the numerical match that the Joads make with Jesus and his disciples: there are twelve of them in total, plus Casy, with two named Thomas and one John. And Connie's betrayal may be likened to that of Judas, as he abandons the family for the three dollars a day he will be paid to drive a tractor, the equivalent of thirty pieces of silver.

6. Screen and Stage Versions

Of Mice and Men

- Play: rewritten for the stage by Steinbeck, directed by George S. Kaufman and produced by Sam H. Harris. Opened in 1937.
- Opera: composed by Carlisle Floyd in 1969.
- Film: directed by Lewis Milestone and starring Burgess Meredith and Lon Chaney Jnr. in 1939.
- Film: directed by Gary Sinise (who also plays George) with John Malkovitch as Lennie in 1992.

The stage version of *Of Mice* ran for two hundred and seven performances on Broadway, before touring the country with great success. Given that *Of Mice* was written for the stage, it is little wonder that both the Broadway and Hollywood versions remain, to a large extent, faithful to the original. However, it would also be true to say that these versions are closer to one another than they are to the book. Whilst there are minor differences in the dialogue and action throughout, it is the alteration made to the scene in Crooks's room that signals a change in emphasis. Neither Crooks nor Curley's wife enjoy the same level of participation as they do in the novel. In particular, it is the omission of the exchange between the two, where Curley's wife threatens to have Crooks lynched, that stands out. Without this episode, Steinbeck's comment on racism is markedly diluted. Whilst this is a significant loss, it should also be remembered, however, that he always intended the theme of fellowship to be at the forefront of any interpretation. In this sense, both the play and the films remained faithful to his wish.

With an eye to the future, perhaps, the efforts of Brian Harley with

Short Night Films in England are worth a mention. He has produced films of individual scenes from *Of Mice* using dialogue taken directly from the novel. This is, of course, in keeping with Steinbeck's idea of a *Play-Novelette*. It is also significant that one of the scenes filmed was the gathering in Crooks's room. Even in a low-budget, small-scale production, the difference is palpable. The racial and gender based tensions are brought to the fore, with Curley's wife balancing victimhood and lethal menace in equal measure. Perhaps the time has come for a fully-fledged retrospection. Let us take another look at Steinbeck's original project, abandoned as it was after sixteen nights in pre-war San Francisco.

The Grapes of Wrath

- Play: adapted by Frank Galati in 1988. Winner of the *Tony Award* for Best Play in 1990.
- Opera: composed by Ricky Ian Gordon, with libretto by Michael Korie, it premiered in 2007.
- Film: directed by John Ford, produced by Darryl F. Zanuck, with screenplay by Nunnally Johnson, in 1940. The recipient of two *Academy Awards*.

John Ford's film is a remarkable cinematic event that captures the *zeitgeist* of 1930s America. We are aware that censorship pressure was not confined to the book alone and it is testimony to Darryl F. Zanuck, who was not known for his radical sympathies, that the commitment to Steinbeck was honoured and the film completed.

John Ford brought to the story of the migrants the vast panoramas of his U.S. Cavalry trilogy. In black and white, the tonal contrasts emblematize the polarization of society as the Joads move Westwards. The unusual structure of the novel, with its contextualizing *intercalary* chapters, does pose specific problems for the filmmaker. However, the cinematic qualities intrinsic to the novel, the reliance on surface detail in place of an obtrusive narrator, and the episodic quality of Dialogism, are features which more than compensate.

7. Bibliography

Bloom, Harold, ed. *John Steinbeck's 'Of Mice and Men'* (Bloom's Guides). New York: Infobase, 2006. Whilst it could be said that Professor Bloom is not the strongest advocate of John Steinbeck's writing, this guide does contain excellent contributions to the ongoing critical discussion.

DeMott, Robert, ed. *Working Days: The Journals of 'The Grapes of Wrath' 1938–1941.* New York: Penguin, 1989. A precious insight into Steinbeck's writing process.

Heavilin, Barbara A., *John Steinbeck's 'Of Mice and Men': A Reference Guide.* Westport CT: Praeger, 2005. An attempt to establish a serious critical frame for reading Steinbeck. There is a thorough discussion of theme, character, style and context and the point is made the *Of Mice* is a text which polarizes opinion.

Heavilin, Barbara A., ed. *The Critical Response to John Steinbeck's 'The Grapes of Wrath'.* London: Greenwood Press, 2000. A valiant attempt to draw a line beneath the factional bickering that has marred much of the discussion about this book. There is a wealth of comment on the subject, from contemporary newspaper reports to a specially commissioned postmodernist analysis.

Karson, Jill, ed., *The Greenhaven Press Literary Companion to American Literature: Readings on 'Of Mice and Men'.* San Diego: Greenhaven Press, 1998. A collection of nineteen essays with an introduction and contextualization by Jill Karson.

Parini, Jay, *John Steinbeck: A Biography.* London: Reed Consumer Books, 1994. A popular biography containing a satisfying amount of information on Steinbeck's life.

Steinbeck, John, *The Harvest Gypsies: On the Road to 'The Grapes of Wrath'*. Berkeley: Heyday Books, 1988 (1936, *San Francisco News*). The series of articles produced by Steinbeck for the *San Francisco News* in 1936. The material from which Steinbeck created *The Grapes* but considered also to be a classic in its own right.

Steinbeck, Elaine and Wallsten, Robert eds., *Steinbeck: A Life in Letters*. New York: Viking, 1975. In a writing style very different to that of his prose fiction, Steinbeck gives the inside story of his remarkable life to friends, family and business associates alike.

Wartzman, Rick, *Obscene in the Extreme: The Burning and Banning of John Steinbeck's 'The Grapes of Wrath'*. New York: Public Affairs (Perseus), 2008. An insight into the controversy surrounding the novel, the threat it carried for the big growers, and the encouragement it gave to the downtrodden everywhere. There is a detailed account of the struggle to resist the banning of the book in Kern County, California, an appraisal of the wider political situation and working class resistance of the time, and a discussion of Steinbeck's methods for the collection of material for his writing.

Watkins, Tom H., *The Great Depression: America in the 1930s*. Boston: Little Brown and Company, 1993. A magisterial, though readable account of this tumultuous period in American history.

About this Book

This is a generously contextualized and uncompromisingly objective commentary on two of Steinbeck's most widely read novels.

Contemporary circumstance is particularly relevant to these classic books—*Of Mice and Men* is a timely warning about fascism, and *The Grapes of Wrath* is an emblem for the oppressed in Depression-era America—so a significant proportion of this study is given over to the framing of social, economic and political context.

It includes a survey of the more prominent critical approaches to the texts, and particular emphasis is given to the importance of Steinbeck's relationship to Modernism. It also offers an insightful, dialogic reading of the books that is both accessible and clearly signposted throughout.

The Author

David Hallard, has an MA from the University of Sussex, which he attained as a mature student. His research interests to date include the fiction of Joseph Conrad and poetry of Edward Thomas. His future projects will include more work on John Steinbeck.

Humanities-Ebooks

All Humanities Ebooks titles are available to Libraries through Ebrary

Some Full Length Literary Titles

Sibylle Baumbach, *Shakespeare and the Art of Physiognomy*
John Beer, *Blake's Humanism*
John Beer, *The Achievement of E M Forster*
John Beer, *Coleridge the Visionary*
Jared Curtis, ed., *The Fenwick Notes of William Wordsworth**
Jared Curtis, ed., *The Cornell Wordsworth: A Supplement**
Richard Gravil, *Romantic Dialogues: Anglo-American Continuities, 1776–1862*
Richard Gravil, *Wordsworth's Bardic Vocation, 1787–1842*
Richard Gravil, *Wordsworth and Helen Maria Williams; or, the Perils of Sensibility*
John K Hale, *Milton as Multilingual: Selected Essays 1982–2004*
Simon Hull, ed., *The British Periodical Text, 1797–1835*
John Lennard, *Modern Dragons and other Essays on Genre Fiction**
C W R D Moseley, *Shakespeare's History Plays*
Paul McDonald, *Laughing at the Darkness: Postmodernism and American Humour **
Colin Nicholson, *Fivefathers: Interviews with late Twentieth-Century Scottish Poets*
W J B Owen, *Understanding 'The Prelude'*
Pamela Perkins, ed., *Francis Jeffrey's Highland and Continental Tours**
Keith Sagar, *D. H. Lawrence: Poet**
Reinaldo Francisco Silva, *Portuguese American Literature**
William Wordsworth, *Concerning the Convention of Cintra**
W J B Owen and J W Smyser, eds., *Wordsworth's Political Writings**
The Poems of William Wordsworth: Collected Reading Texts from the Cornell Wordsworth, 3 vols.*
* These titles are also available in print using links from
http://www.humanities-ebooks.co.uk

Humanities Insights

These are some of the Insights available at:
http://www.humanities-ebooks.co.uk/

General Titles

An Introduction to Critical Theory
Modern Feminist Theory
An Introduction to Rhetorical Terms

Genre FictionSightlines

Octavia E Butler: *Xenogenesis / Lilith's Brood*
Reginal Hill: *On Beulah's Height*
Ian McDonald: *Chaga / Evolution's Store*
Walter Mosley: *Devil in a Blue Dress*
Tamora Pierce: *The Immortals*
Tamora Pierce: *Protector of the Small*

History Insights

Oliver Cromwell
The British Empire: Pomp, Power and Postcolonialism
The Holocaust: Events, Motives, Legacy
Lenin's Revolution
Methodism and Society
Risorgimento

Philosophy Insights

Adorno
Agamben
American Pragmatism
Barthes
Thinking Ethically about Business
Critical Thinking
Existentialism
Metaethics
Contemporary Philosophy of Religion
Philosophy of Humour
Philosophy of Sport
Plato
Žižek

Literature Insights

Made in the USA
Las Vegas, NV
24 March 2022